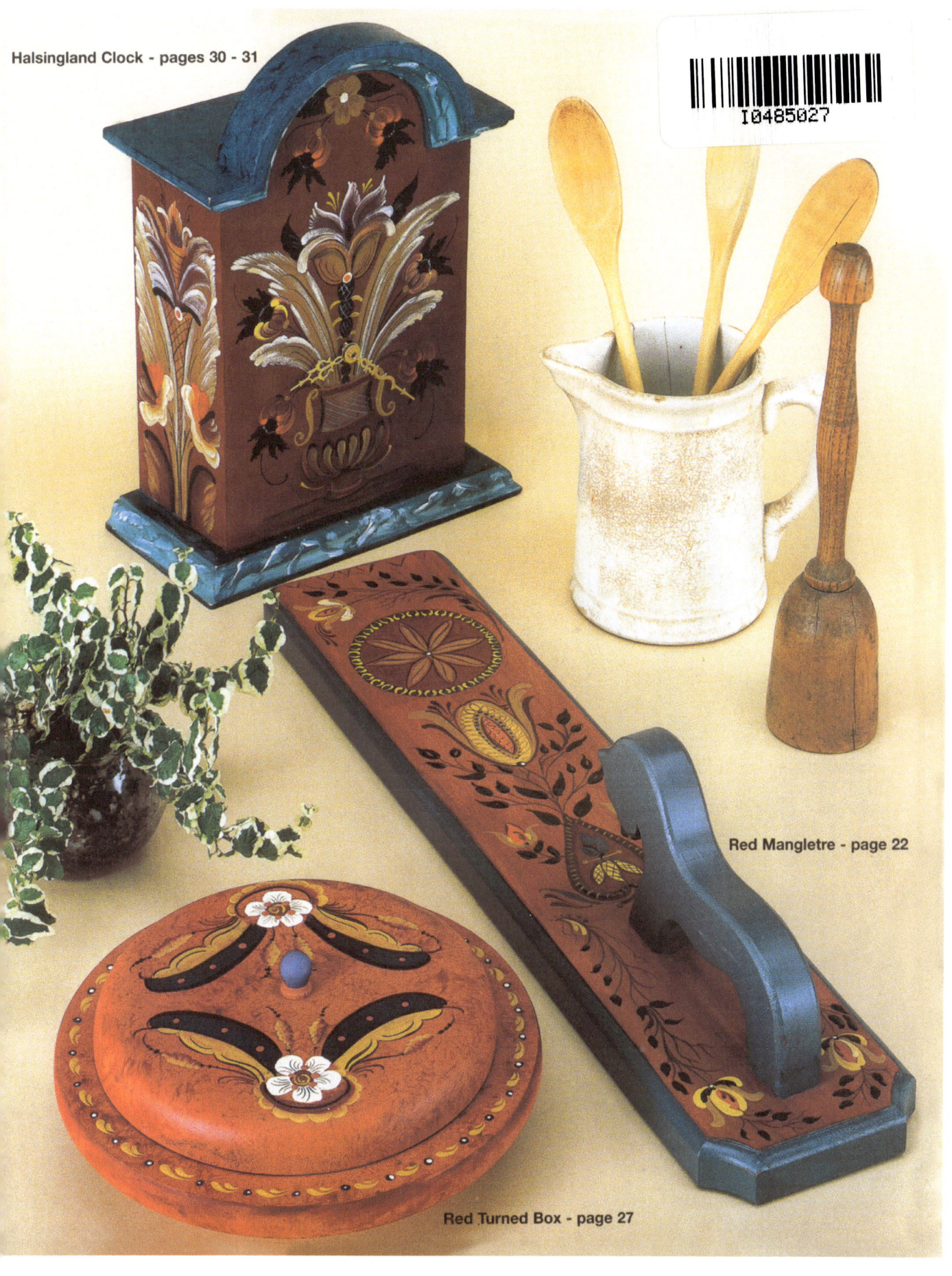

Halsingland Clock - pages 30 - 31

I0485027

Red Mangletre - page 22

Red Turned Box - page 27

DESIGN BASICS FOR
SWEDISH FOLK ART
VOLUME 1

SWEDEN

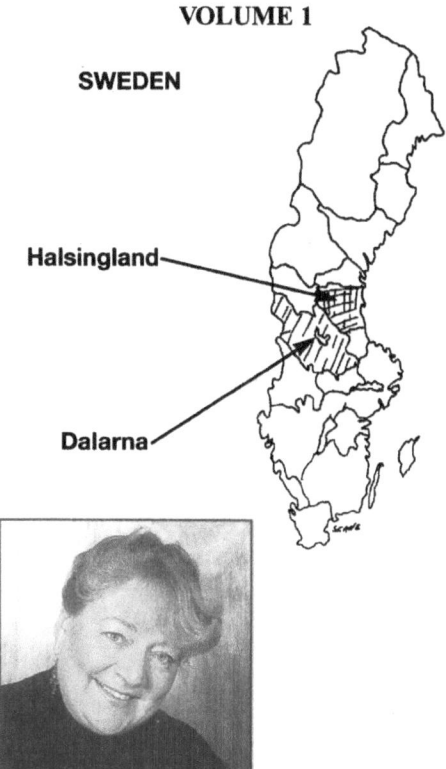

Halsingland

Dalarna

BY DIANE EDWARDS

This Swedish Folk Art Volume 1 is the third book in the Design Basics series. The first two books were on Norwegian Rosemaling, Telemark Style. I have a BS and MA degree in Art Education and have had a business, Rosemaling and Crafts since 1976. This book is dedicated to my staunch supporter, our daughter, Liesl in her graduation year! Congratulations!

LESSON PLANS
This book is set up like the other Design Basics books to allow teachers to follow a logical lesson sequence for teaching Swedish Folk Art. A seven or eight week lesson sequence follows.
1. Introduction to Swedish Folk Art and History
2. Typical patterns, supplies, colors
3. Basic strokes
4. How to paint kurbits
5. How to paint flowers
6. Borders
7. Background techniques and colors
8. Adding details and accents

INTRODUCTION

This book is an introduction to the beautiful Swedish folk art produced during the 1700's to about the middle 1800's. Development was greatest in Central Sweden and down into the southern areas. This Folk Art painting was known as "Rosnaling", which means "decorative painting" in Swedish. Although the name is similar to the Norwegian "Rosemaling", the painting is entirely different and the Swedish art form has its own national characteristics. Swedish painting was done in wooden items, directly on walls and ceilings, and on canvas or paper which was attached to the walls. Sometimes the painting was attached permanently as wallpaper and other times hung for special occasions and then stored.

This exciting art form can be easily learned to decorate your home or that of others. The Swedish Folk Art Exhibit which will be touring the US and Canada through 1997 has evoked a new interest in Swedish Folk Art. The book, "Swedish Folk Art: All Tradition is Change" accompanies the exhibition and is a valuable addition to your library. See Bibliography.

Research undertaken while writing this book produced a few older books and lots of reprinted photos and colored illustrations but little "how-to" information. To translate this folk art into today's paints and colors took a little more time than I had anticipated, but I hope that you enjoy the book and find it a practical addition to your Folk Art Library. In this space I have covered only a taste of each of these designs and styles and will hope to cover more information in the future.

My research mainly involves the provinces of Sweden known as Dalarna, Halsingland, Harjedalen and down into Central Sweden. Works of art are found all over Sweden but were not necessarily

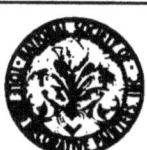

Would you like to meet people who share the same love of painting as you? Become a member of the NSTDP. For more information write: NSTDP • P.O. Box 808 • Newton, Kansas • 67114

Copyright © 2010 Diane Edwards
All rights reserved.
ISBN: 1453876863
ISBN-13: 9781453876862

painted in the provinces where found. Some wooden pieces were constructed in one area and then painted by an artist in another. Experts in Swedish folk art recognize the carpentry of different provinces since it is stylized like the painting is.

In the province of Dalarana there were various schools of painting which can be recognized. There were certain artists-- sometimes families, including women, who did a lot of commission work and had a distinctive style. Some of these schools were the Leksand school and the Rattvik school, these can be identified by the coloration, type of design motifs used, and ways of arranging their designs on the canvas or space painted. There were several painters--up to forty--recognized in each school.

The wall paintings usually depicted Biblical scenes with the people and buildings presented in contemporary ways, an unusual presentation in most folk art. This made the art work more appealing, interesting and certainly, more Swedish. Many of these are quite happily depicting scenes such as the Crucifixion and other stern lessons from the Bible in a colorful, enjoyable manner. The Scandinavians, always pragmatic about religion and royalty--after all didn't they change from time to time?--used the only pictorial references they had.

Although some of the wall paintings were from other printer's plates, most of them came from the Gustavus Adolphus Bible published in 1618. "Figure Bibles" were published throughout the 1700's using these illustrations. The foremost researcher of Dala painting is Svante Svardstrom whose doctoral thesis in 1949 confirmed the source of the Dala paintings. (See Bibliography.)

Considering the age of many of the paintings in Sweden it is interesting that so many have survived. Some have been found turned around to face the wall as the practical Swedes used the back of the canvas for wall paper, insulation and simple wall covering. Some of the painted furniture pieces have, unfortunately, been stripped. Whenever I see a piece of bleached and stripped Scandinavian pine in an antique shop, I shudder. Thankfully, in the last 25 years painted furniture has become more popular. Recently an antique shop in Denver sold a beautiful painted Swedish armoire for $12,000. Further imports of valuable painted furniture sometimes follow and some of these should be in museums to be enjoyed by thousands. Since most painting of the type known as "kurbits" was not done much after 1875 the pieces are increasingly rare. They must be treasured and preserved as an important part of our heritage. I hope that this little book helps you to understand and enjoy this wonderful Folk Art.

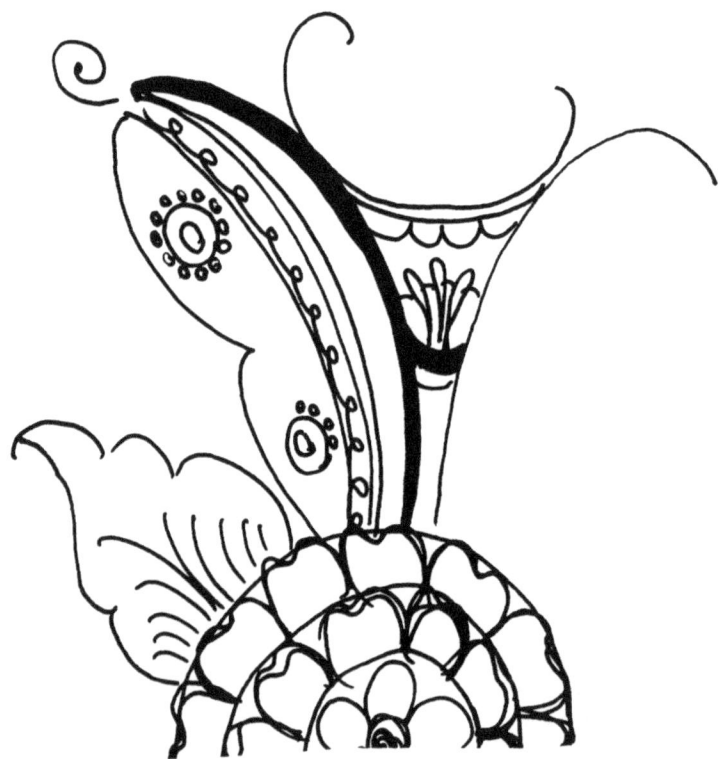

HIS-STORY

In the long, cold dark of winter in Sweden the folk artist prepared his colors--yellows and golds for the sunshire and warmth of the day; blues for mysticism and trueness of heart. The purplish blues of royalty and power, reds for trueness, loyalty and the Blood of Christ. This painting would be of the Resurrection--it would be his best yet. He had prepared the canvas with several coats of milk paint--a casein mixed with whiting and chalk that made the canvas glisten and gleam. He had taken this order on his summer trip up into the Norther Provinces last year. He knew the farmers well, he had painted a canvas for them last year of the Crucifixion. They were good people who would pay him a nice fee.

The canvas was about eight feet long and four feet wide. He had taken careful measurements last summer. The family wanted their fest room to be the finest in their area. They were pleased with his work as he painted the largest, most luxuriant "roses" or gourds of any artist. His flowers were beautifully executed and his figures wore the finest of the local dress. He didn't stint on filling his "tapeter" or wall hanging with glorious color and fine borders. He like to draw carefully but paint with feeling and heart--an uplifting painting that would make you feel good when you ventured into the unheated Fest room to remove items from the kiste or chests.

Yes, the man was a true artist--unschooled but skilled in his craft. He was now teaching his children to help him. His daughter was very interested and showed a fine hand in detail and outlining. In fact, next year he would give her a small commission of her own to work on. He needed help as he was not very well--having served as a soldier in the last war. He wasn't able to do much farming and so his art work was his family's subsistence. He was doing well, however, and had commissions for the whole winter almost every year. As people saw the wall paintings that were beginning to fill the wealthier peasants' homes more and more commissions came in.

He began mixing up his colors--he planned on using up the colors in the next few days, so had to plan to keep painting once he started as the casein would spoil.

As he mixed he eyed the beautiful clock he had painted for a rich landowner just last week. He had used linseed oil on this piece and it was very expensive but he had been paid well. The wooden clock, made by a carpenter in Mora, glowed with the rich color of the oil paint--it almost lit up the corner of the small dark house. He smiled in satisfaction and bent to his work. . .Mary's cloak would be blue. . .

PAINTING THE FLOWERS

As with most folk art the strokes are based on the "c" and "s" strokes. I prefer to use the filbert brush as the rounded end makes all the strokes easier. Presumably most folk art was done with a round brush as artist's of that time made their own brushes using cow's or other animal hairs and inserting them into a quill from a feather of some type. These would have had to be quite large for the big brushes that they used for the walls--one would assume that they would wrap them with some type of fine, strong thread and varnish to protect them from water or turps. The finest painters probably would work hardest on their brushes--as we all know--good strokework is not easy even with a wonderful brush!

Use a large enough brush for the item you are painting. One cannot achieve a nice strong stroke with a tiny brush. The brush must be able to lay flat when it is pressed out to lay the paint down without any ridges, etc. I prefer to use a size six, eight or ten unless I am painting jewelry! Because it is much easier to tell if the brush is too large, start with the biggest brush you think you could use and go down from there. The old artists prefered to make one stroke do the work of two. Today we tend to make five strokes do the work of one. This gives a contrived, heavy look to what would be a lively, light painting.

To give rhythm and a little texture I will usually side load the brush and then go back a put a little extra paint on that side. This gives a nice clean edge to the outside of the stroke and keeps excess paint from building up on the inside. Look at the color sheet for stroke examples. When baseing in a flower, I load the brush a little thinly on both sides to avoid extra texture. That can be added in subsequent strokes.

Be sure that you do not go over strokes while they are drying. This leads to nasty little holes and other problems like balled up paint. I always prefer to wipe off a stroke (use baby wipes) if I think it's so bad I'll have to reshape it. When doing two coats always let the paint dry thoroughly between coats. Do your strokes from the outside to the inside. This builds the flower or leaf shape in the way the old folk artists did. Since they would have painted most of their pieces free-hand, that natural build-up of strokes looks correct.

Although perfection is an admirable trait sometimes folk art can look so perfect as to be DEAD. This is not the way your work should look. In our present day society we work so hard to make everything right and correct and perfect that any artistic qualities that were there to start with are gone. Make your strokes as good as you can and let them lay there. If they look too bad, wipe them off and start over. Practice to make the best possible strong, clean strokes.

Swedish flowers on the kurbits are usually fairly open and airy on light backgrounds. You can let the background show through or keep the centers light in color. (The canvas or wall painting was done in a lighter manner than the wood painting which was usually dark, compressed--or close together and edged with lighter colors to give definition. We will explore this style in the chapter on wood kurbits.)

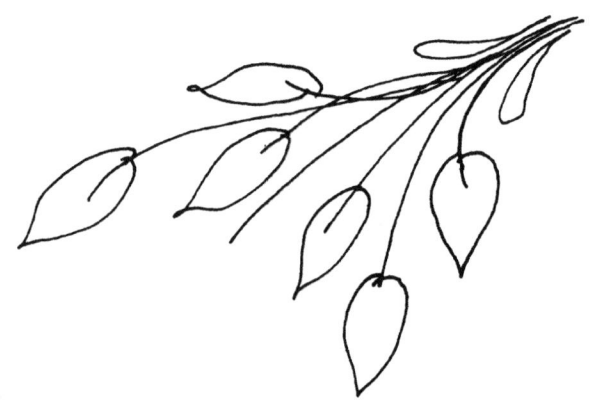

DESIGN MOTIFS

Illustrations used were often from the printing plates of the time. The floral vines, borders and other decorative motifs came from the Renaissance florals that were used to illustrate books and printing plates of the time. These usually involved an urn or pot of some type that this floral arrangement grew out of. Over time the urn became smaller and less important and the vine itself grew into a bouffant display as large as some garden! The kurbit is a gourd or cucumber vine. The Biblical reference is to Jonah as he was recovering from his grief outside Nineveh. In the book Swedish Folk Art, authors Hellspong and Klein say on Page 34, "In modern times it has been called a gourd after the name of the bush that grew over Jonah. . .But kurbits was a learned name; the people called it a rose." The word "kurbits" came from the term "cucurbita" which is a gourd vine. Whatever the historical description, the kurbits are unique to Swedish Folk Art and are a glorious and beautiful extension of the floral tradition.

MOTIFS used by Swedish artists included hearts, bows, swags, long floral rows with leaves that often go off in straight lines. They used as fillers small floral bouquets or plants, a flower known as a spinette that is long, spiral shape that grows out from the kurbit design.

ARTISTS SCHOOLS

Certain artists and "schools" painted their floral arrangements differently; colors, unusual arrangements and personal style variations. However, a certain design similarity can be found in most of these florals. They are based on the univeral folk art strokes of C's and S's. They grow gracefully from a central point, sometimes an urn, sometimes a hand--albeit a bouquet that would topple over most people! The lines of the stems and leaves follow through in a graceful arc of C and S strokes. Sometimes they are on a straight line but the flow of the whole design has grace and beauty. This probably explains why so many of these rather gigantic works of art have been preserved for over 100 years.

Swedish wall paintings are usually fairly open and airy. There is white or light background showing through that gives space to the design. In the wood painting the background color--such as rusty red--is used as one of the colors of the design and the flower is shaped by edging the brush with paint. Added definition on either was done with the liner brush. Like the Norwegian rosemaler, the Swedish artist was quite adept with the outlining or detail brush. On an almost crude depiction of a building you will see intricate detailing of scrolls and florals. Of course there may have been two people working on some of these wall paintings, also. Many of the paintings were executed at home during the long winters and the orders were taken the summer before. This meant that any family member, including women, could work on the painting. Unlike other folk art many of these paintings were signed or can be attributed to a school of artists, which makes identification easier.

PAINTING MEDIA

The Swedish folk artist used several different types of paint. Paintings which were done on wood were usually done with oils. Earlier painting may have been done with egg tempera, casein, or distemper. Distemper is a pigment mixed animal glue or fish glue. This mixture could be unstable but many wall paintings done with it have lasted. Egg tempera, while a very stable, long-lasting medium also is very slow drying and would probably be done more on wood than canvas panels. Casein--a mixture of buttermilk and pigment would have been the best choice for most wall panels. The disadvantage to this paint is that it keeps for only a few days--making remixing a constant chore. Although the early linseed oil and pigment mixtures were also ground by hand they had the advantage of long storage possibilities. The decline of folk art began after oil paints came out in tubes--partly because the folk artist used too many colors. The greatest strength of Swedish folk art is in its coloration; fewer colors create better design, better tonality throughout the painting and fewer value changes except in the focal area. Several hundred years of wear, tear and "antiquing" with dust and smoke have simply mellowed some of these pieces to a beautiful patina. The colors must have been quite strong initially to have survived the ages. The lack of Cadmiums left the reds and yellows softer and more compatible with other colors. When these colors became available they were so expensive that most artists only used small touches of them. This kept the colors quite mellow and soft, with highlights and color notes that moved the eye throughout the painting in a gentle and enjoyable manner.

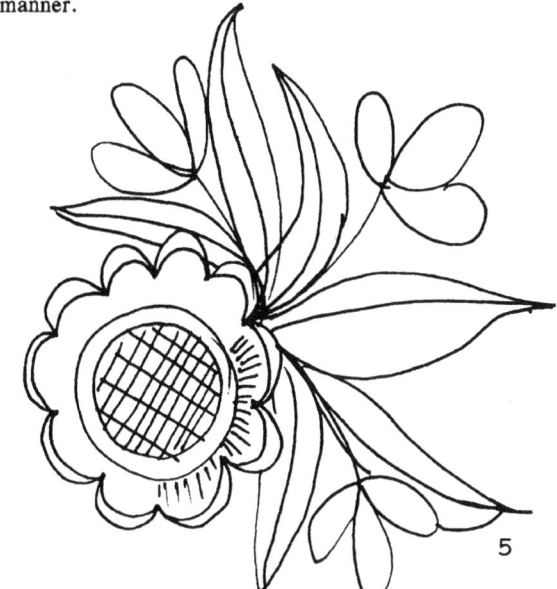

5

SWEDISH WOOD DESIGN

Scandinavian carpenters were especially talented with wooden furniture and armoires were their favorite showcase. Usually these armoire's have an interesting "bonnet" top that is sometimes overpowering to the rest of the piece. These were usually painted with assorted types of borders and the compressed kurbits. Often painted dark red or reddish brown, dark green or the Scandinavian favorite Baltic Blue, they dominated the small rooms of the peasant houses. Many of the clocks were quite large and had this bonnet top, also.

Another wood piece which is typically Swedish is the Mora clock which was made in Mora in Dalarna. This clock has a round moon face and is shaped something like a woman with large hips. It is typically painted--sometimes Ivory or White, but usually the colors above. These were usually decorated with kurbits or compressed kurbits. There are several which have vine florals and other more classical motifs.

The book, The Decorative Arts of Sweden, by Iona Plath has some interesting clocks, armoires and chests pictured. This book was written in the 1940's and is still available and very informative book on Swedish Folk Arts.

Chests in central sweden often had flat lids--some of the other areas had the usual rounded top associated with Scandinavian trunks. They were often tapered from top to bottom--a seaman's trunk. Often long bands of iron held these tops together and the iron work could also be quite exquisite.

Carving was done extensively on almost all the different wooden articles constructed during the long winters and Swedish carvers executed beautiful work. Sometimes the carving was also painted, sometimes only the flat surfaces. Lots of pieces originally painted have been stripped today. Most wooden items were identified as to owner, dates and sometimes, the artist. Almost everything was decorated in some manner. If not with paint, with carving, woodburning or incising. Early patterns were lines, circles, dots, C or S shapes and geometric shapes. Geometric shapes were the first decoration used--plant forms came later in the Renaissance.

Although the basic scroll that comprises so much of Norwegian rose-maling was known to Swedish artists they rarely used the scroll prefering the more decorative vine and leaf forms. The borders were also used in Sweden more than in Norway. The urns and vases of the Renaissance became less opulent and eventually became a small part of the Kurbits designs--sometimes disappearing altogether. The pine cones, ribbons, wreaths, shells, foliage, swags and flowers integrated into the particular Swedish style of the times. In the cities the Neo classical style became the rage. The Gustavian style of pale washes of color, clean white and ivories has remained popular in Sweden to this day. Viewed in the home of Carl Larsen and other artists it has been emulated all over Sweden and become known as the Swedish style. The clean, pale decoration with the use of painted panels trimed with borders of fluting, frets, beads of the Neo Classical style has remained a favorite to this day.

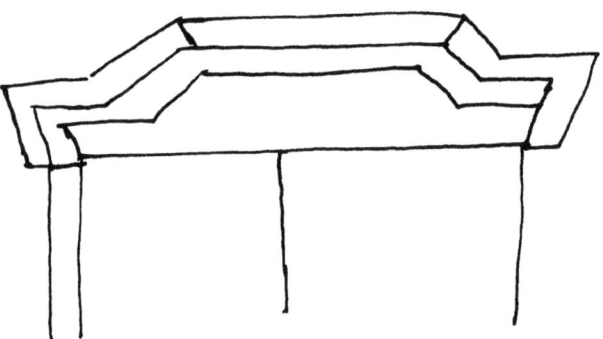

Bonnet Armoire

PAINTING THE KURBITS

The kurbits are a type of leaf in the design or the term can also mean the design itself. In this discussion I will be talking about the kurbit as a leaf shape. The kurbits grow on the gourd or pumpkin vine--there are also other leaves that are around the kurbits and the flowers. These leaves are usually blue or green while the kurbits are often painted half light and half dark. The light side is sometimes painted in gold such as Yellow Ochre while the dark side is sometimes dark Green and sometimes dark Blue. There are many variations, of course, depending on the artist. Some of the artists painted their own interpretation but in general you can tell where some of the paintings are from by the way the kurbits are done. The Leksand school had strong kurbits outlined with dark blue or brown or black. The Mora and Rattvik school often had just plain green leaves. An artist of either school has their own style which often changes quite radically when painting on wood instead of the canvas. However, many of these pieces are signed or have been identified so can be compared and studied. As time went on the kurbits became more abstract and kind of became a swirl of strokes instead of a leaf.

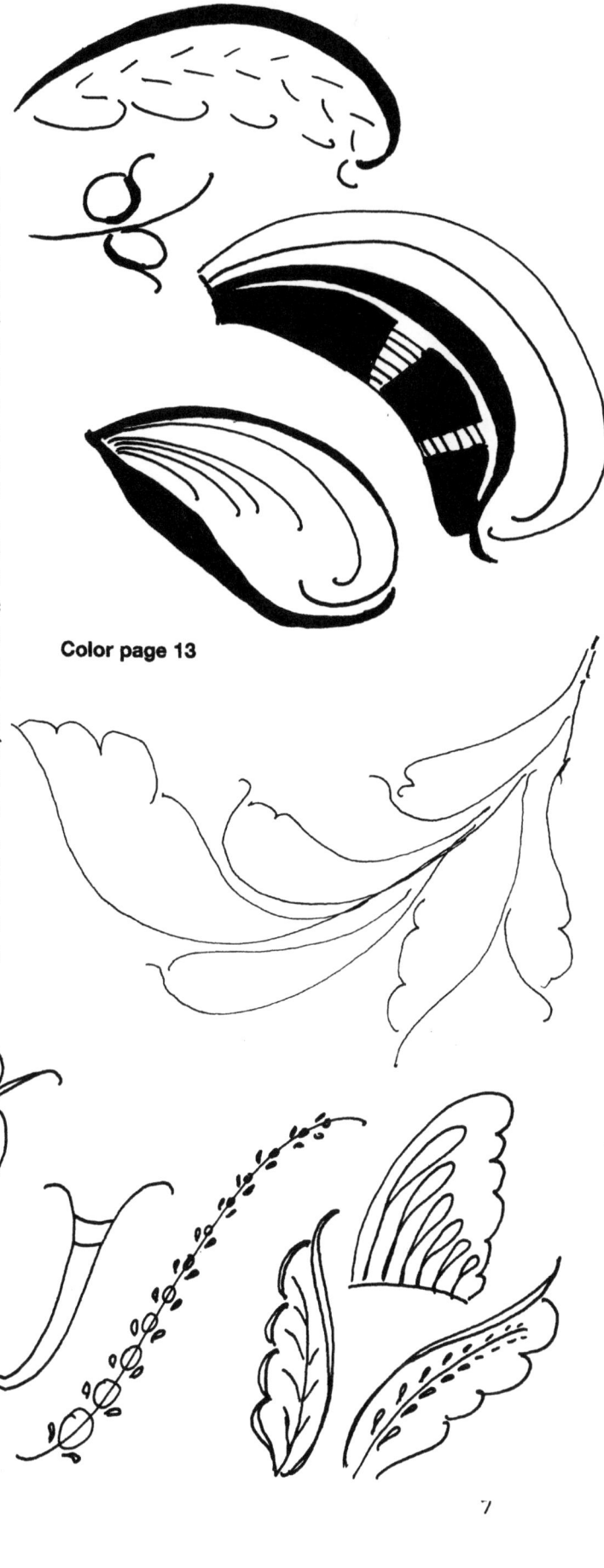

Color page 13

Basic Strokes

The basic strokes for Folk Art are the C and S strokes, using the filbert or a flat brush if you prefer. These strokes are easily accomplished with the filbert because it has a rounded edge.

LOADING

Dip brush in water, load with juicy paint — stroke brush first on one side and then on the other to flatten the brush. This gives you a sharp chisel edge. Be careful not to remove all your paint. When painting a stroke always hold the brush with one hand and prop up that arm with the other. This is the BEST stroke art painting position. You will be able to support a strong, deliberate stroke which is well-controlled.

THE STROKES

The C stroke: Hold the brush upright as you press down firmly at the beginning of the stroke. Press the brush down all the way at the beginning of the stroke and then start to lift while pulling through the stroke. At the end of the stroke the bristles return to a chisel edge. Illustration 1.

The S stroke is painted by holding the brush vertical on its chisel edge. Angle the brush on a diagonal line and slowly press down until the brush is fully extended and then start gradually easing up as you pull the brush back on to its chisel edge. Illustration 2.

WHEN **DOUBLELOADING,** load the brush fully. Stroke it on the palette to remove any extra paint on the edge of the brush. Then, reload the paint side of the brush in a contrasting color. Stroke once on the palette to blend so that you have a blended edge, not a hard line of color.

Illustration #1
Fibert Stroke

Notice the hand over hand technique and upright handle of the brush. The brush is extended fully for this stroke and then brought up towards yourself lifting to the chisel edge.

This stroke gives a rounded end to the stroke and finished with a chisel edge line. To load this stroke it is important that you have at least half of the brush loaded with paint.

LINER STROKES

Load the brush in thinned paint fully, stroking through the paint pulling the brush towards you — never stroke away from yourself with the liner. Twist the point of the brush on the dry palette paper pulling the brush towards yourself. This creates a fine point on the brush. The brush will have a rounded area of paint all the way up to the ferrule. You can then do lines or teardrops with the same brush.

The "secret" to making fine lines is 1) Load the brush fully, 2) Use your other hand to support your painting hand, 3) Hold your brush about an inch above the ferrule, and 4) Hold your brush straight up and down and work just with the tip. Start your liner moving in the direction of the line BEFORE you actually touch down and then follow through slightly AFTER you actually lift it up. This gives a rhythmic movement to your work and since all lines must flow from the root it keeps your design moving correctly.

TEARDROPS

Are done by loading the liner brush and positioning your arms the same way as for lines. However, when you make a teardrop your brush assumes a 45 degree angle. IF your brush is not fully loaded your teardrops will end in a point. Look at the examples of teardrops. Notice how they all follow a line from the stem line or from the root. No teardrops or linework exist independently of the flow of the main design. All linework follows through on the design flow lines of the rest of the design elements.

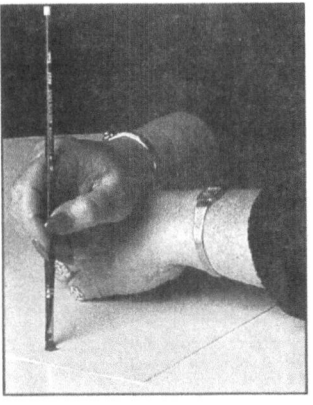

Illustration #1

8

Illustration #2
Chisel Edge Stroke

Notice the height of the hands on this stroke and the vertical handle on the brush. It is important that you draw the brush down towards you and have the right arm extended to have room to pull that stroke.

Illustration #3
Side Loaded Stroke

Load the clean, slightly wet brush on one side and stroke on your palette to achieve an even transition of paint from heavy to nothing. I also squeeze the brush on the clean side to get rid of any water that would make a line. Lay the brush down, pushing out the side with the paint on it to allow the brush to lay flat and show the shaded edge.

Illustration #4
Liner Brush Stroke

It is important not to try to make a line without the support of your other hand. Use this hand-over-hand technique to give much better control of the liner. Also, twist your liner in the thinned paint until you have it loaded to the ferrule. Then, twist the point on the palette paper to start with a fine line. The liner must be vertical to do a fine line. Any angle will cause it to splay out.

Illustration #5
The Teardrop Stroke

Teardrops are made two different ways.

One—a fine, long teardrop in made by loading the brush as for lines, starting with a fine line and laying the brush down. This is the Norwegian teardrop and is used at the ends of lines in the kurbits and in flowers. Your brush will be at a 45 degree angle to the paper.

Two—the comma stroke is made by loading the clean brush heavily at the end with fresh paint and laying down the paint. You pull the brush out slowly towards you to achieve the fine tail.

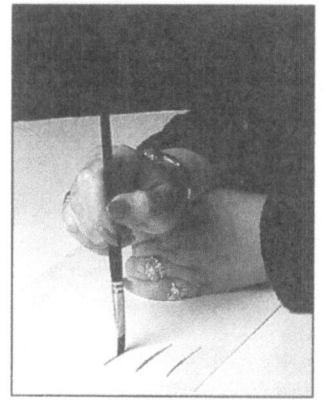 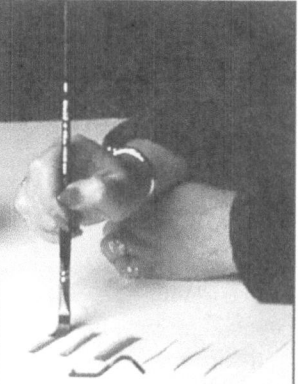

Illustration #2　　　　　Illustration #3

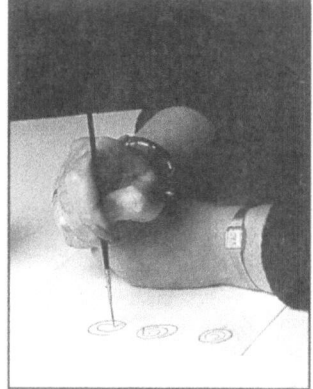 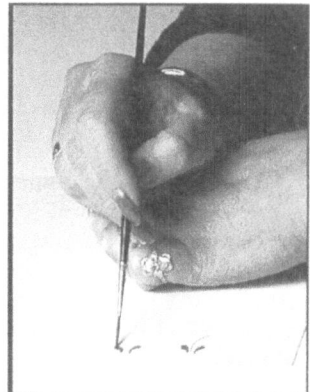

Illustration #4　　　　　Illustration #5

Brushes Used In Book

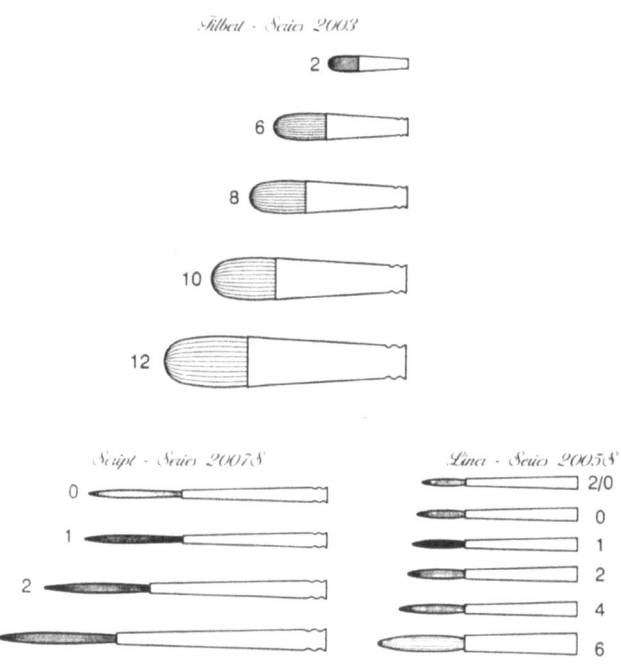

Filbert - Series 2003

2
6
8
10
12

Script - Series 2007S

0
1
2
4

Liner - Series 2005S

2/0
0
1
2
4
6

9

SWEDISH BACKGROUND COLORS AND TECHNIQUES

GLAZING:

To produce an antique Swedish look I prefer to paint very thinly and then to use glazing or lazuring on my pieces. This does not show too well on the photographs as they tend to show less depth, however, each of the pieces for this book has been glazed in some fashion. The Swedish dyes are still popular for wooden pieces. This can be simulated by mixing in JS Retarder or Deco Brush N' Blend into the paint as you apply it. These products do not produce a sealed wood surface so if you want this to be sealed you can brush on a thin coat of JS Clear Glaze. The end product should show visible wood grain. The idea is to keep the wood from being so thickly coated so as to look like plastic. Wood graining gives an old, rich look to the piece. The glazes used over each background color are listed with the piece.

METHOD:

Use a large flat or angle synthetic brush. Sponge brushes don't work well for this. Load the brush with Retarder and load with a little paint. You will go back and reload paint as you go. Be sure and paint with the grain. The final product should not look tinted but rather painted with the wood grain showing slightly. This can be recoated when warm to the touch if you feel it is too thin. I always start out too thin and work up. You can wipe off the paint with a baby wipe and start over, but who wants to? After this backgrounding is dry, I brush on a thin coat of JS Clear Glaze. I have also used Deco Control Medium-it is a little thicker so add a few drops of water. When this is dry--20 minutes or so, I load the brush fully in JS Retarder and touch the corner of my angle brush in the colored glaze. I use blue on blue, red on red and yellow oxide on golds--these should be mixed to match your backgrounds--blue and red and yellow oxide make browns. The idea is to enhance and deepen the first backgrounding. Sometimes it gets too heavy--you may have to wipe off with a baby wipe, but usually picking up a little retarder will work it out.

TEXTURE:

For the textured glazing or lazuring I use Deco's Control Medium or JS Kleister Medium. I use a paper towel or rag squished together and then loaded with the Medium. Use a styrofoam plate so that you have enough room. Put the texture on FIRST with the clear mediums and then touch the glaze on the towel and start with that. That gives you much better control of the color. This can be redone over and over again until you are satisfied. Remember to let some of the original color show and not to get the second color on too thick. That way you get the depth you are looking for. A varnish will enhance this effect. Try sponges, combing (I like to cut notches in cardboard), your fist--a popular Swedish trick--cut potatoes or carrots or anything that will produce texture and not leave unwanted lint or chemicals

ANTIQUING:

On the edges of pieces I often try to get a little darker "antique" look. You can achieve this by letting the first coat dry and then use the Retarder and add a darker shade to the edges with the large angle brush. For example: on a red background I will use a red glaze with a touch of blue in it to darken it. The new Heavenly Hues from DecoArt work really well as glazes, also. I use Earth Brown, Shadow Tan, Hunter Green, Soft Black and Heavenly Gold--colors which give the Old World look I want. These stay wet a long time and are really easy to work with. My motto is: never leave a background color plain without some enhancement--besides it's so much fun to play with!

To antique OVER the painting: Paint on a coat of Clear Glaze and let dry. Use JS Retarder and paint over an area that is fairly easy to handle at one time. Paint on your antiquing color--you can use the JS glazes or the Deco Heavenly Hues for this for maximum control. Wipe off areas you want high lighted. Use a good paper towel or rag so that you don't get lint into the painting. Wipe and repaint as necessary. The slowness of the drying time combined with retarder gives you a lot of time--but--don't introduce water into the mixture or you will have trouble as water makes the retarder dry much faster--it tends to grab the paint and set up.

SPATTERING

This is done a great deal in Sweden on walls and furniture. Use an old brush--I like about a size 8 flat--load with a little water and a little juicy paint. Hold out the index finger of your left hand and flip the brush down over it until you see the spatters start to fall. Wipe off any bad ones immediately and keep on until it is covered evenly. In Sweden they use White, Black and any colors--this makes for very strong spatters!! Whole walls, wainscoting and doors are often done this way.

MARBLIZING

Undercoat with White or a light color. Side load a Filbert Brush in a size that fits the area. See clock marblizing. Side load first in Retarder and work it into the brush well--then side load into Blue. Do a shaky stroke at an angle to simulate marble. I like to use an old brush so that the loading gets a little streaky. Pick up a little Burnt Sienna with a liner and do a few lines with that and Retarder. Last pick up some White with a liner and Retarder and do lines with that. Some of the Swedish marbling is Clouds marbling and some has circular marbling--see Bibliography for complete books on these techniques.

BORDERS AND EDGES

A piece that has any border definition at all should be painted a contrasting color.

The usual combinations are Red with Blues or Greens, Greenish Blues with Golds, Reddish Browns with almost any color background. Traditional combinations are Blue Haze with Red Iron Oxide, Deep Midnight Blue with Tomato Red, Napa Red with Antique Teal, Hauser Green Deep with Georgia Clay or True Ochre--shaded with Raw Sienna. I use Antique White or JS Smoked Pearl and JS Primrose or Deco Yellow Ochre on many of my pieces. These colors are very typical of old Swedish colors. Burnt Sienna is a good border color with lighter reds, or any of the blues or greens.

NOTE: (If you do your painting with oils on these acrylic backgrounds you will have much better success if you brush on a coat of JS Clear Glaze before using the oil paints. You may do your backgrounding glazing with either acrylics or oils using a linseed oil or 1-2-3-Glaze. I use Pale Drying Oil from Weber Permalba--a wonderful quick drying medium with little odor.)

Borders used by Swedish artists were really intricate and beautiful. They were masters of the border techniques. Some of the artists had signature borders that identified their work. Some of the "schools" also used the same or similar borders that help to identify their work.

When you plan your painting it is a good idea to plan for the border in the very beginning stages so that it looks like part of the over all design of the piece. Be sure to carry your color scheme over into the border so that the color moves all around the whole piece.

Keep your border area smaller than the overall design area so that it doesn't overwhelm your design. Your eye should go to the design area first and then the border. You can also grey the border by glazing it very lightly with a thinned grey or antique it with a thin glaze of brown.

ACCENTS used by the Swedish artists were sometimes linerwork, teardrops, small stamped designs using potatoes or wooden stamps, or stencils. The stencils were often cut to allow easier repetition of certain elements such as urns, vases, scallops, or border elements that went all around a room. A stencil could be intricate or simple depending on the artist. Some artists used their stencils over and over and so their work can be identified. Stencils were used mostly on walls however, not as much on furniture which were usually painted freehand.

Some of the artists were very good draughtsmen in a time when brushes were not so good and masking tape hadn't been invented! Some of the straight lines they achieved were probably made with a dagger striper brush, and a ruler. The dagger striper brush is a long knife-like brush that has a short handle and has to be dragged towards one. It takes a little getting used to, but when mastered is very efficient in doing long, straight lines.

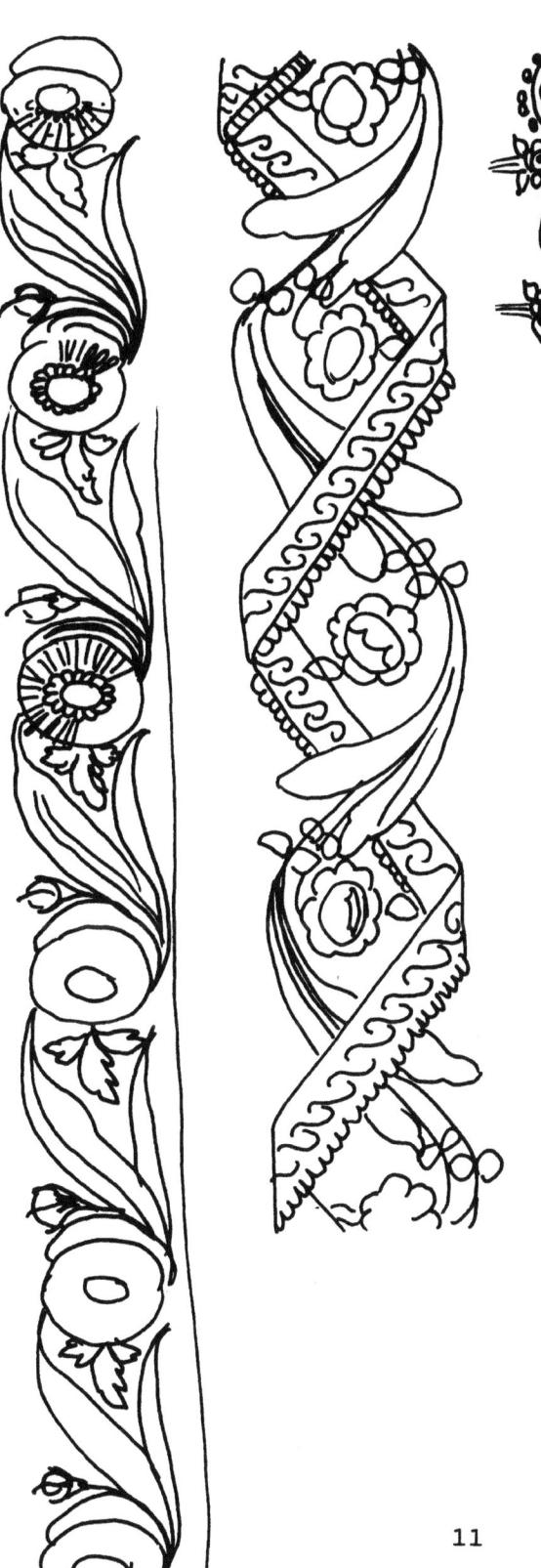

CONVERSION CHART

DECOART	JOSONJA
Titanium White	Titanium White
Antique White	Smoked Pearl

YELLOWS

Yellow Ochre	Primrose or Yellow Oxide plus T. White
Golden Straw	Yellow Oxide + Yellow Light + tch. White
Sand	Yellow Oxide 1 pt White 5 pts
True Ochre	Yellow Oxide 1 pt, White 5 pts plus a touch Yellow Lt.

REDS

Cadmium Orange	Vermillion
Tomato Red	Napthol Crimson
Napa Red	Burgundy + touch Napthol Crimson
Cranberry Wine	Burgundy
Raw Sienna	Raw Sienna
Georgia Clay	Norwegian Orange
Red Iron Oxide	Red Earth
Burnt Sienna	Burnt Sienna

BLUES

Sapphire	Sapphire
Blue Haze	Sapphire 2 pts + Teal Green 1 pt
Blue Mist	Sapphire + Teal Green + White
Antique Teal	Teal Green
Deep Midnight Blue	Storm Blue

GREENS

Hauser Dark Green	Pine Green
Hauser Med Green	Pine G + W + Yellow Lt.
Hauser Lt Green	Pine G + W + more Y. Lt.
Soft Black	Burnt Umber + Carbon Black

BASIC PALETTE FOR SWEDISH PAINTING
VALUE LIST

Titanium White
Soft Black
(PUT OUT WHITE AND BLACK ALWAYS, NOTE THAT THIS BLACK IS A DARK BROWN.)
Lights to dark for each color.
YELLOW
White--light for yellow
Golden Straw--Mid Value Yellow
Raw Sienna--Dark Value Yellow
Burnt Sienna--Darker Value Yellow
RED
Golden Straw or White--light
Red Iron Oxide--Mid Value Red
Cranberry Wine--Dark Value Red
BLUE
Blue Mist--Light
Blue Haze--Mid Value Blue
Deep Midnight Blue--Dark Value Blue
GREEN
Hauser Lt Green (or Golden Straw)--Light
Hauser Med Green--Mid Value
Hauser Dark Green--Dark Value

This is a sample palette for ideas-- you would change colors for different backgrounds. EX: Blue Haze is better on Greenish Blue backgrounds, Sapphire better on Grey Blue backgrounds. Experiment with color to get your favorites.

TIP-- I use a styrofoam plate with a wet paper towel on it, covered with a piece of deli paper. This stays wet for a long time especially when placed in a plastic bag while not painting.

TIP-- Place paint used with a liner brush on a clean dry plate. This paint should always be fresh or your linework will suffer. I put a small cap of JS Flow Medium on this plate for finer lines. Swedish painting uses lots of teardrops, also, best done with fresh paint.

Leaves and Kurbits Worksheet

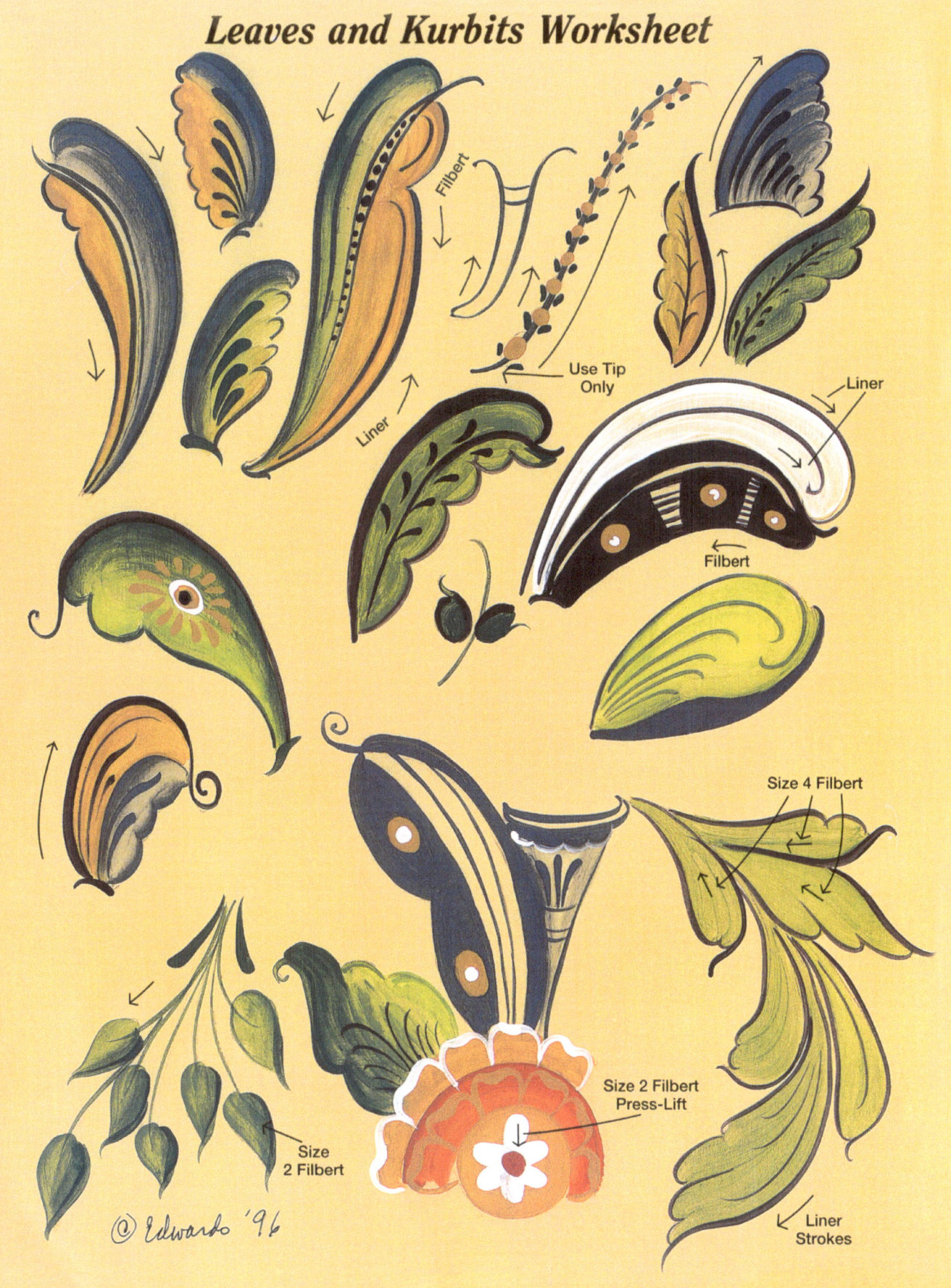

Filbert

Use Tip Only

Liner

Liner

Filbert

Size 4 Filbert

Size 2 Filbert

Size 2 Filbert Press-Lift

Liner Strokes

© Edwards '96

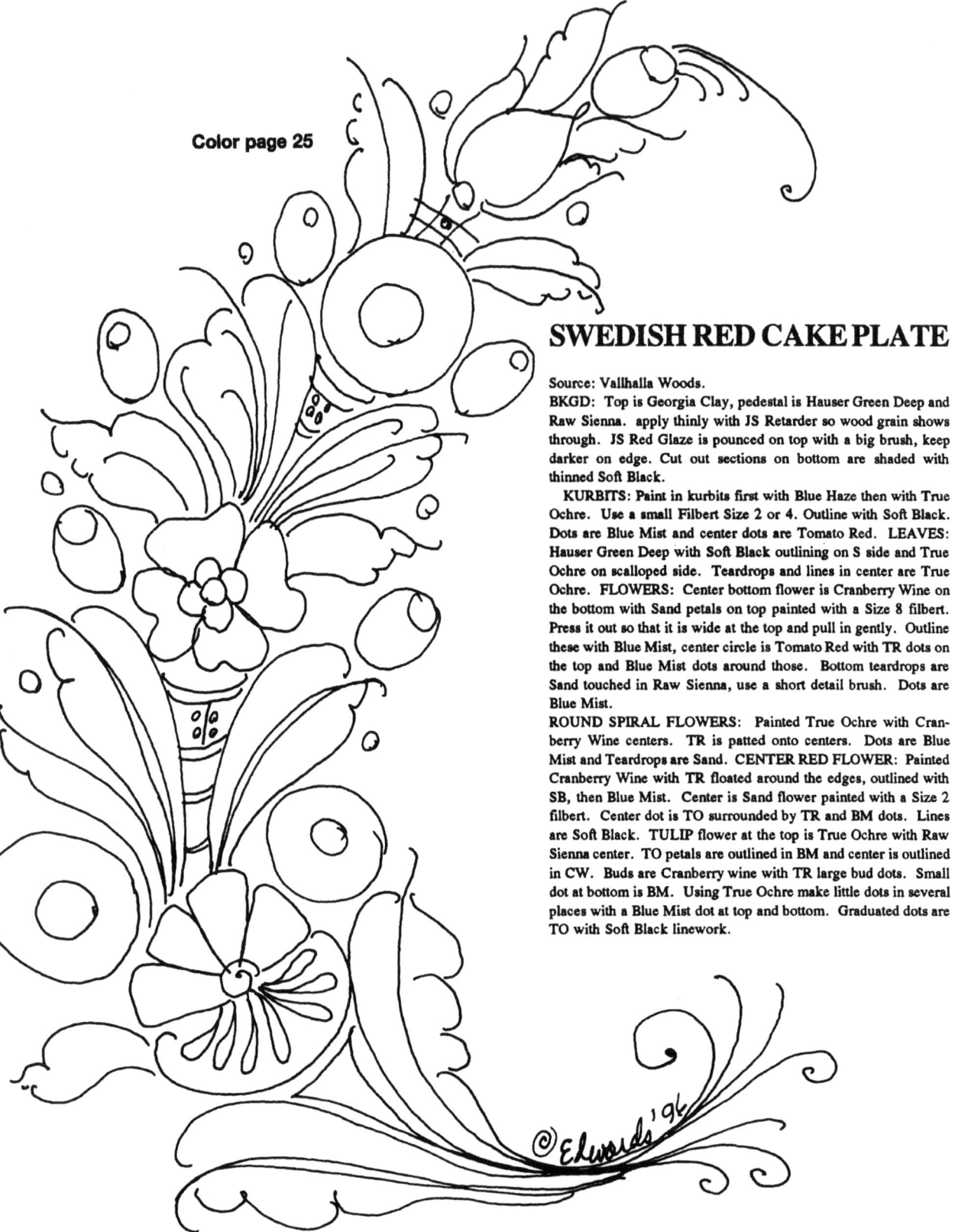

Color page 25

SWEDISH RED CAKE PLATE

Source: Vallhalla Woods.

BKGD: Top is Georgia Clay, pedestal is Hauser Green Deep and Raw Sienna. apply thinly with JS Retarder so wood grain shows through. JS Red Glaze is pounced on top with a big brush, keep darker on edge. Cut out sections on bottom are shaded with thinned Soft Black.

KURBITS: Paint in kurbits first with Blue Haze then with True Ochre. Use a small Filbert Size 2 or 4. Outline with Soft Black. Dots are Blue Mist and center dots are Tomato Red. LEAVES: Hauser Green Deep with Soft Black outlining on S side and True Ochre on scalloped side. Teardrops and lines in center are True Ochre. FLOWERS: Center bottom flower is Cranberry Wine on the bottom with Sand petals on top painted with a Size 8 filbert. Press it out so that it is wide at the top and pull in gently. Outline these with Blue Mist, center circle is Tomato Red with TR dots on the top and Blue Mist dots around those. Bottom teardrops are Sand touched in Raw Sienna, use a short detail brush. Dots are Blue Mist.

ROUND SPIRAL FLOWERS: Painted True Ochre with Cranberry Wine centers. TR is patted onto centers. Dots are Blue Mist and Teardrops are Sand. CENTER RED FLOWER: Painted Cranberry Wine with TR floated around the edges, outlined with SB, then Blue Mist. Center is Sand flower painted with a Size 2 filbert. Center dot is TO surrounded by TR and BM dots. Lines are Soft Black. TULIP flower at the top is True Ochre with Raw Sienna center. TO petals are outlined in BM and center is outlined in CW. Buds are Cranberry wine with TR large bud dots. Small dot at bottom is BM. Using True Ochre make little dots in several places with a Blue Mist dot at top and bottom. Graduated dots are TO with Soft Black linework.

GOLD HORSE CLOCK

Source: Cabin Craft.
BKGD: Honey Brown Shade edges with Raw Sienna and after this is dry go over with a touch of Burnt Sienna to give more depth. When shading, load your large angle brush first with Retarder and then a little paint.
HORSE: Side load a Size 4 filbert with Raw Sienna and paint horse with heavier side of paint to outside. Let the background paint show through. Tail is Golden Straw and mane is Soft Black. Center heart is Red Iron Oxide with Cranberry Wine shading on one side. These hearts are made with a Size 4 Filbert. Lines are Hauser Green Deep, Golden Straw teardrops and dots are Cranberry Wine. Numbers are True Ochre with Golden Straw for highlight. This clock can be painted with additional teardrops and linework--refer to the color photo. To add details look for the root position of each small design. For instance, the heart can have a root from the top or from the bottom--all lines coming from this root position are C or S strokes. Add teardrops following these strokes.

HEART BOX HOLDER

Source: Allen's Woods.
BKGD: front DECOART Yellow Ochre, Red Iron Oxide on back piece. Glaze on back is JS Red Glaze pounced on with an old brush. Front edges and sides are Raw Sienna mixed with js Kleister Medium and pounced on with a big old brush. After drying thoroughly they were lightly glaze with JS Red Glaze and Retarder.

Back section is painted with Blue Haze dots and Raw Sienna teardrops. Tit. White dots on each corner and on top of RS teardrops.

Front section: Paint in True Ochre tulips and White center flower. Add leaves using Hauser Green Deep, Medium and Light going from one to another for variety. Don't clean your brush. Use a Size 2 Filbert so leaves come to a nice point. Lines are all HGD. Blue Haze tulips and and teardrops are added next. All red hearts, red tulips and strokes on top are RIO. Dot flowers are Tit. White with Blue Haze centers. Teardrops on Red Hearts and teardrops are Raw Sienna.

Color Back Cover

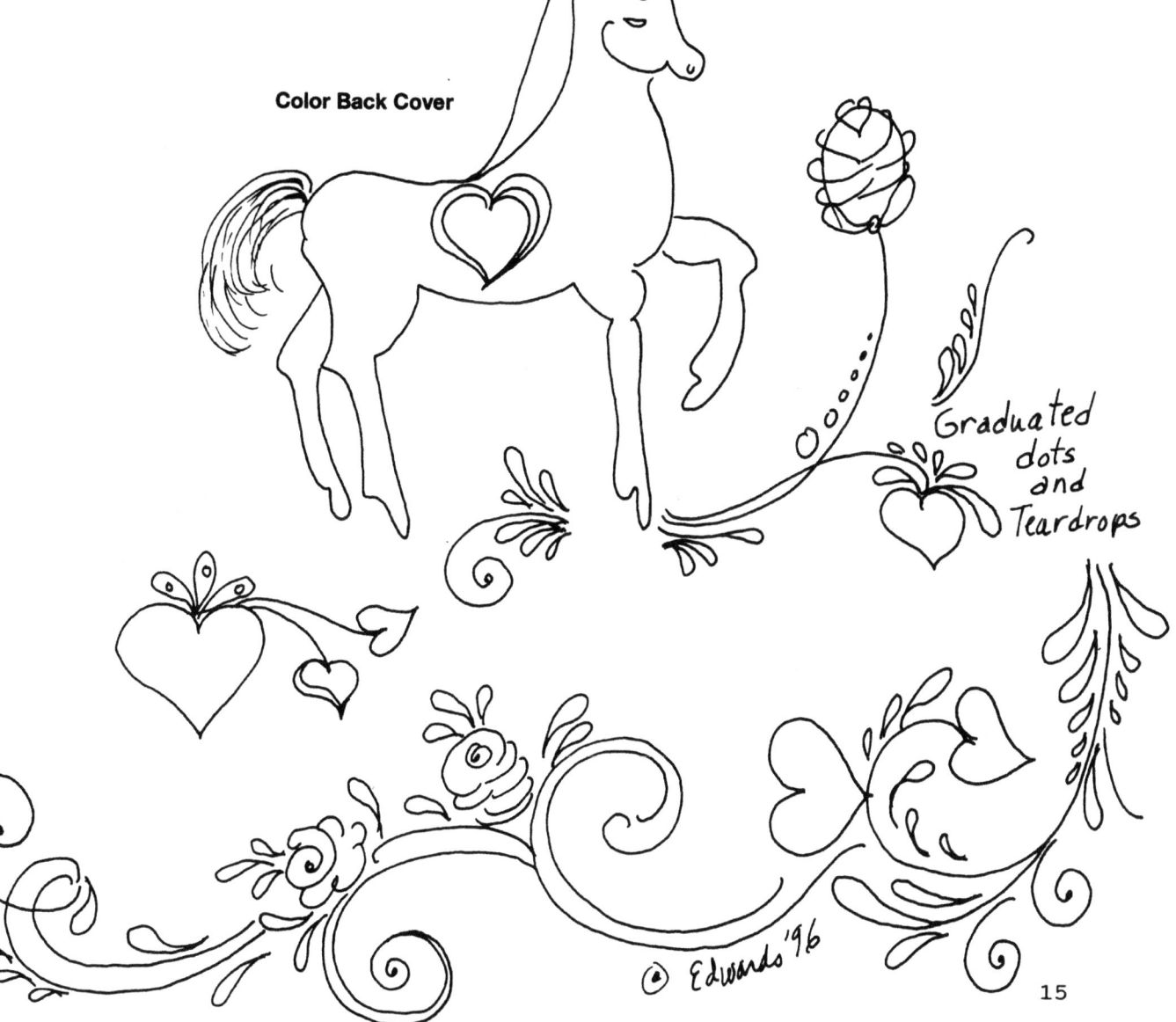

Graduated dots and Teardrops

© Edwards '96

15

Details Worksheet

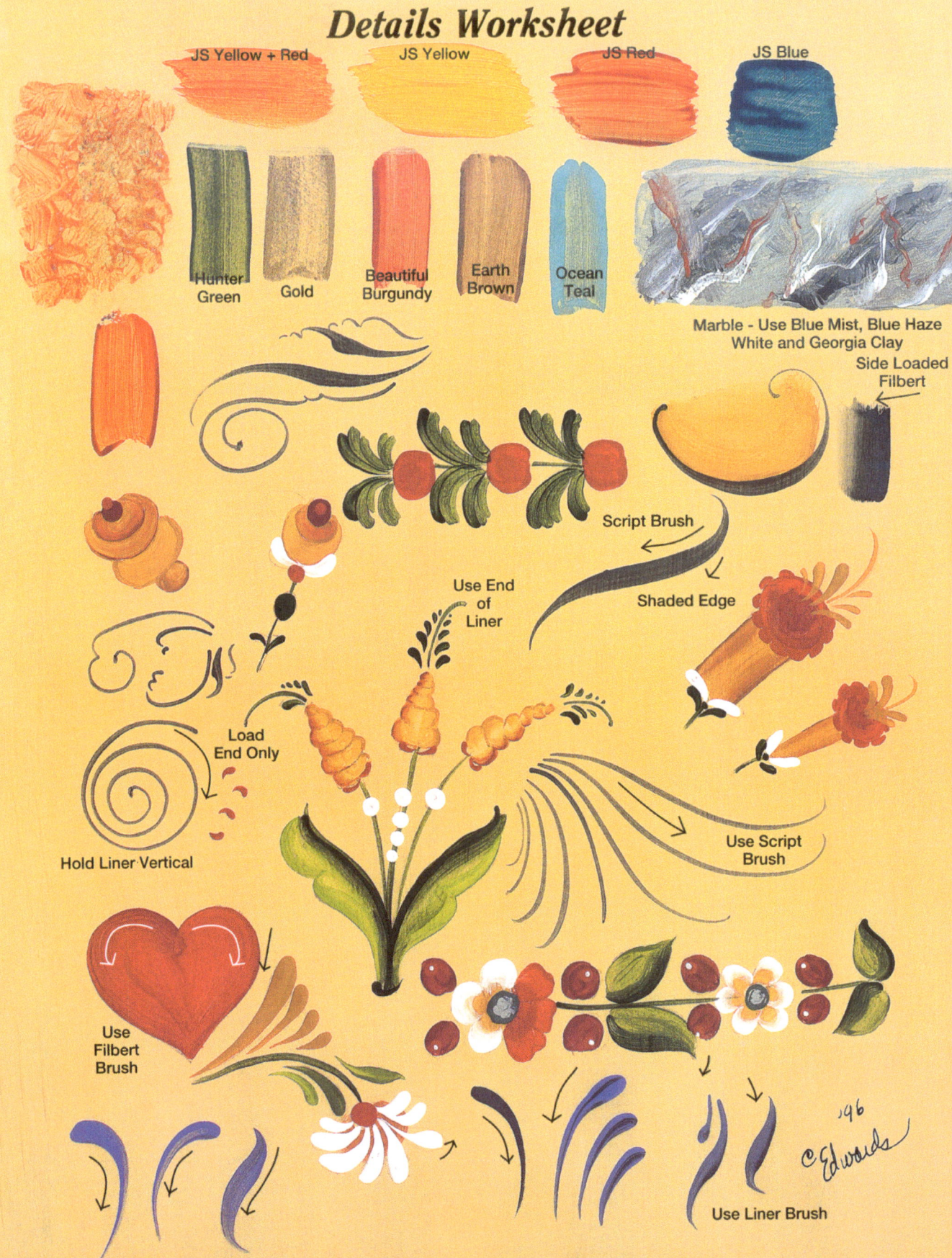

JS Yellow + Red

JS Yellow

JS Red

JS Blue

Hunter Green

Gold

Beautiful Burgundy

Earth Brown

Ocean Teal

Marble - Use Blue Mist, Blue Haze White and Georgia Clay

Side Loaded Filbert

Script Brush

Shaded Edge

Use End of Liner

Load End Only

Hold Liner Vertical

Use Script Brush

Use Filbert Brush

'96
C Edwards

Use Liner Brush

Flowers Detail Worksheet

Deep Midnight Blue

Sapphire

Geogia Clay

Tornato Red

Cranberry Wine

Burnt Sienna

True Ochre

Golden Straw

White

Cadmium Orange

Hauser Dark Green

Hauser Medium Green

Hauser Light Green

Blue Haze

Mix

Blue Mist

Soft Black

© Edwards '96

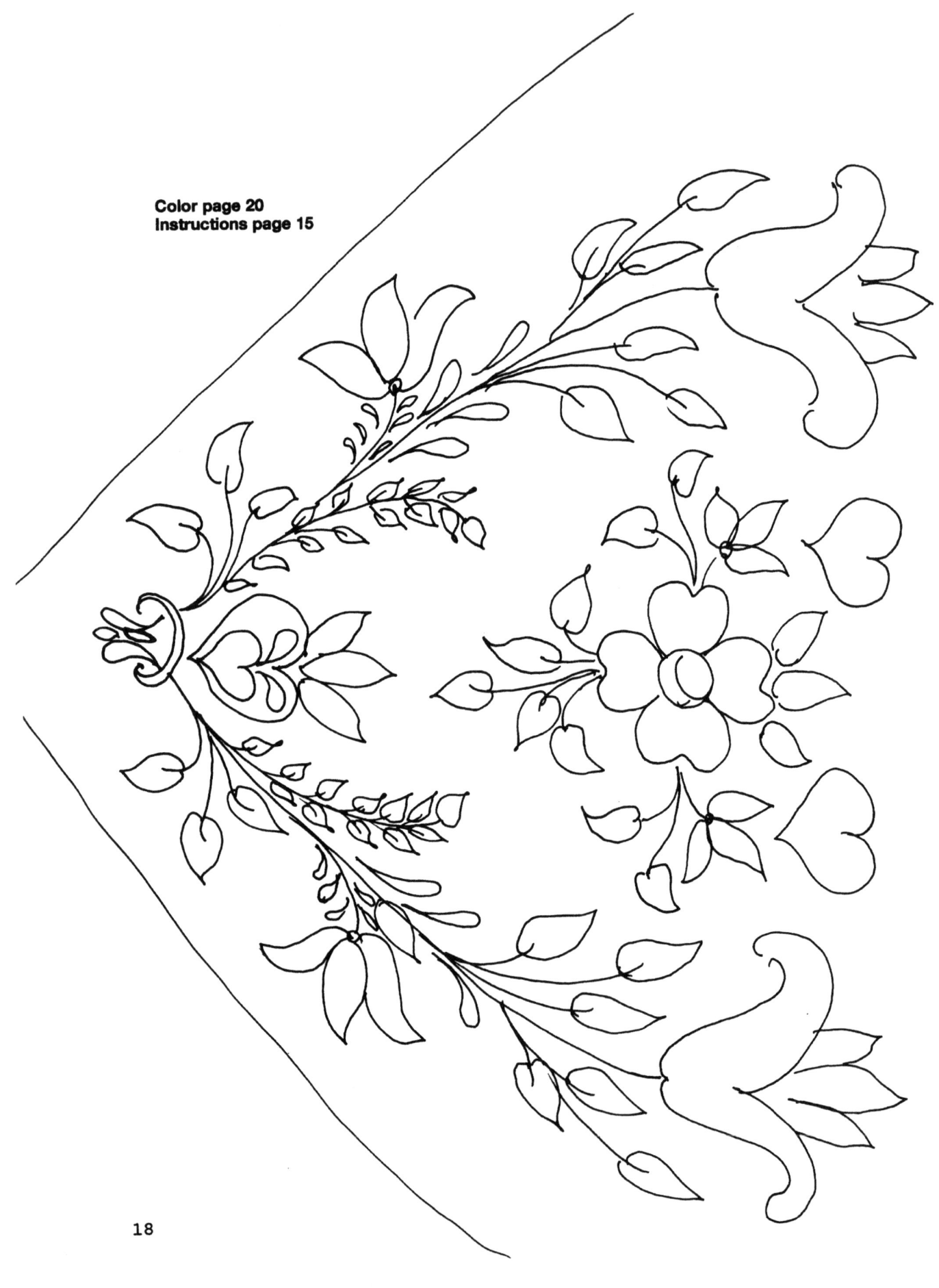

Color page 20
Instructions page 15

18

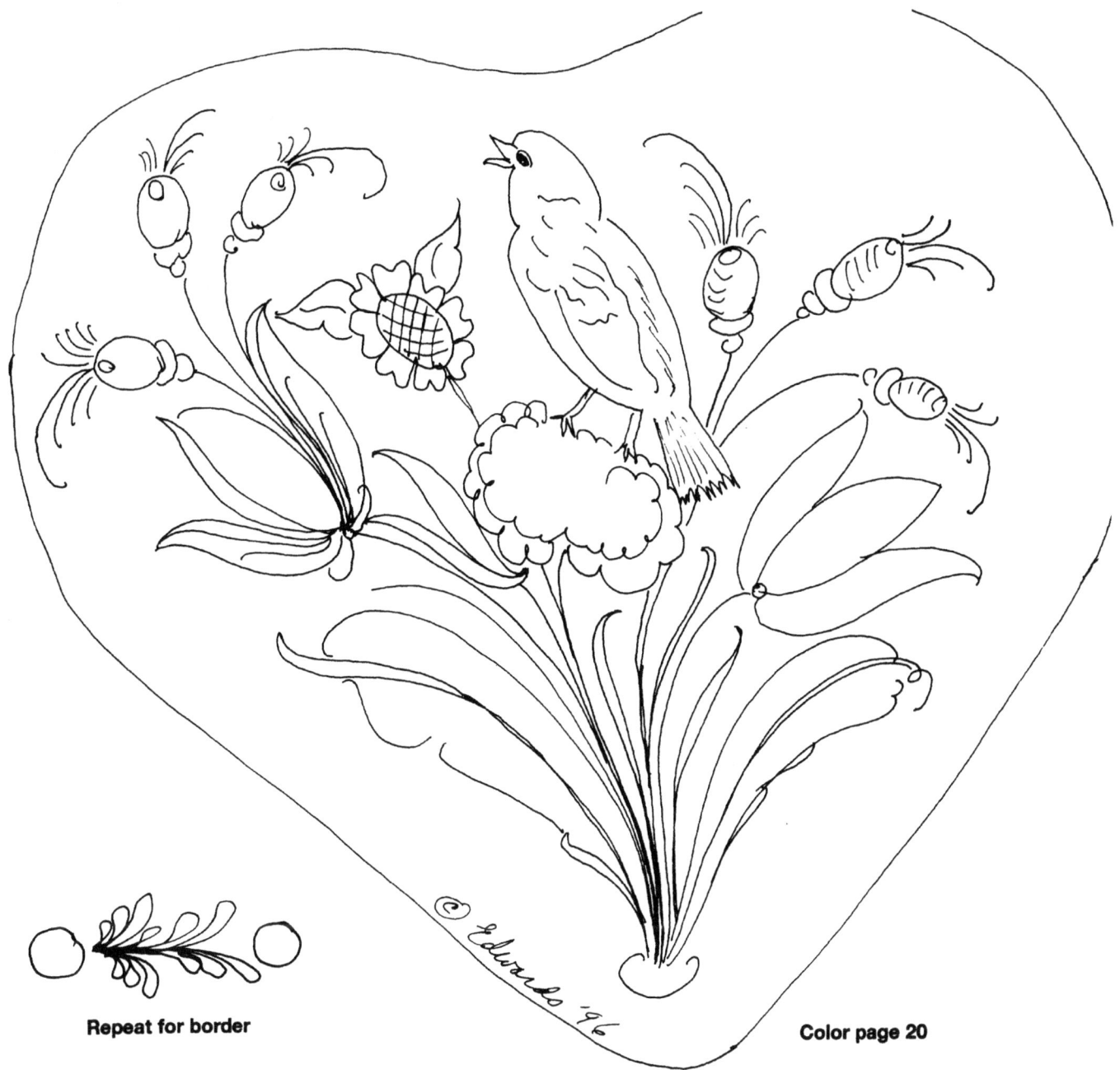

Repeat for border

Color page 20

CREAM HEART BOX

Source: Cabin Craft.

BKGD: DECOART Yellow Ochre.

Glaze with JS Red mixed with JS Yellow Glaze. Edges are Raw Sienna. Border is Napa Red circle finger dots with Hauser Green Deep teardrop style strokes. Use a Size 2 filbert and pull strokes in starting with longest one. See details color page.

KURBITS: Blue Haze on top strokes and True Ochre on bottom. Leaves and grass are Hauser Green Deep. Outline with Soft Black. Bird is Blue Haze thinned slightly with a touch of water. Birds tummy is Georgia Clay. Spinettes are True Ochre edged with floated Georgia Clay and outlined with Soft Black. Sunflower is True Ochre with HGD leaves and a Georgia Clay center. Sides are floated with Napa Red. Parrot tulips are Napa Red painted about two thirds of the way up the petal. Immediately take a Size 4 Filbert with a little Titanium White and dry brush in the White strokes. If it doesn't look dry brushy enough repaint Napa Red and start over. Center carnation is two coats of Napa Red with short little White teardrops.

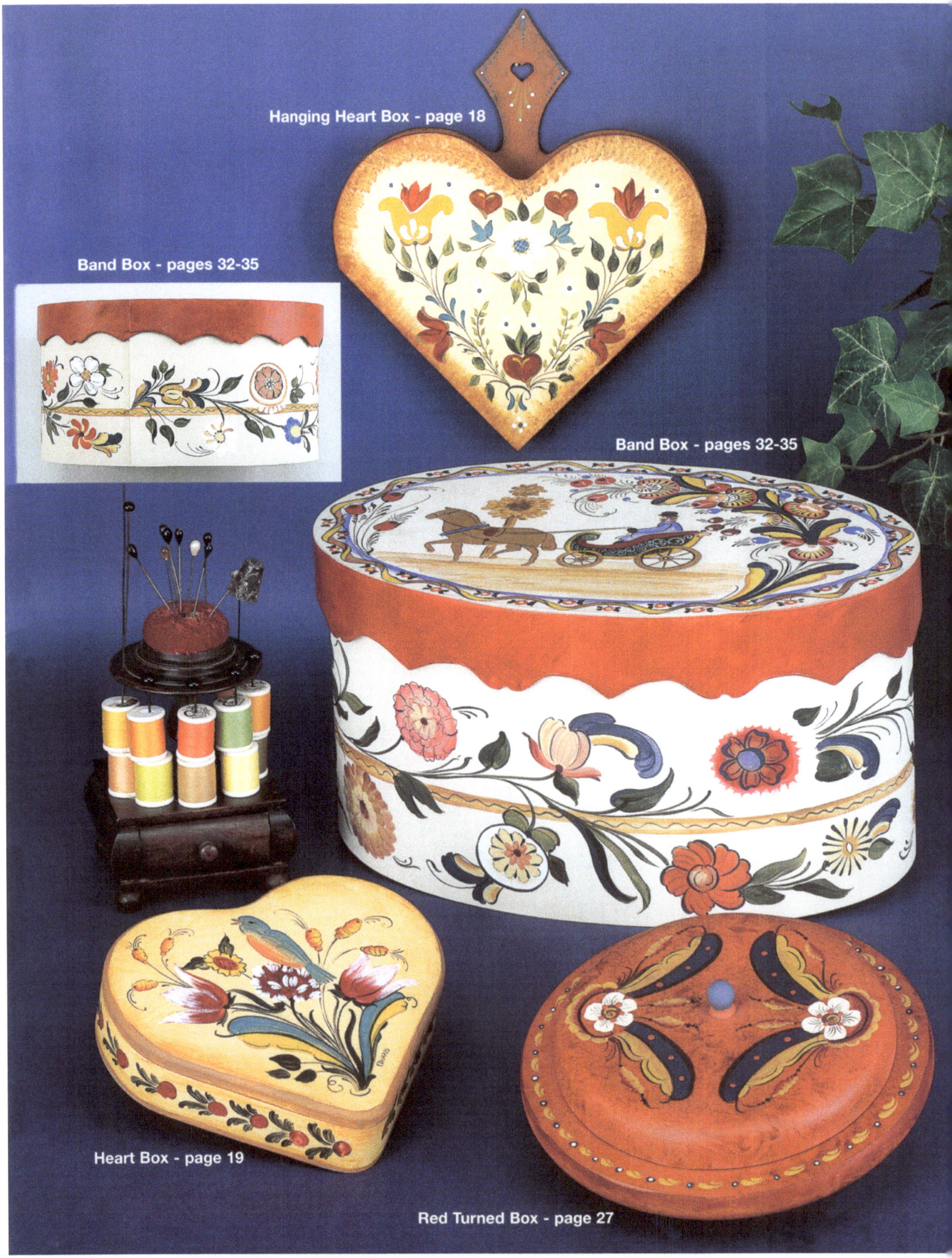

Hanging Heart Box - page 18

Band Box - pages 32-35

Band Box - pages 32-35

Heart Box - page 19

Red Turned Box - page 27

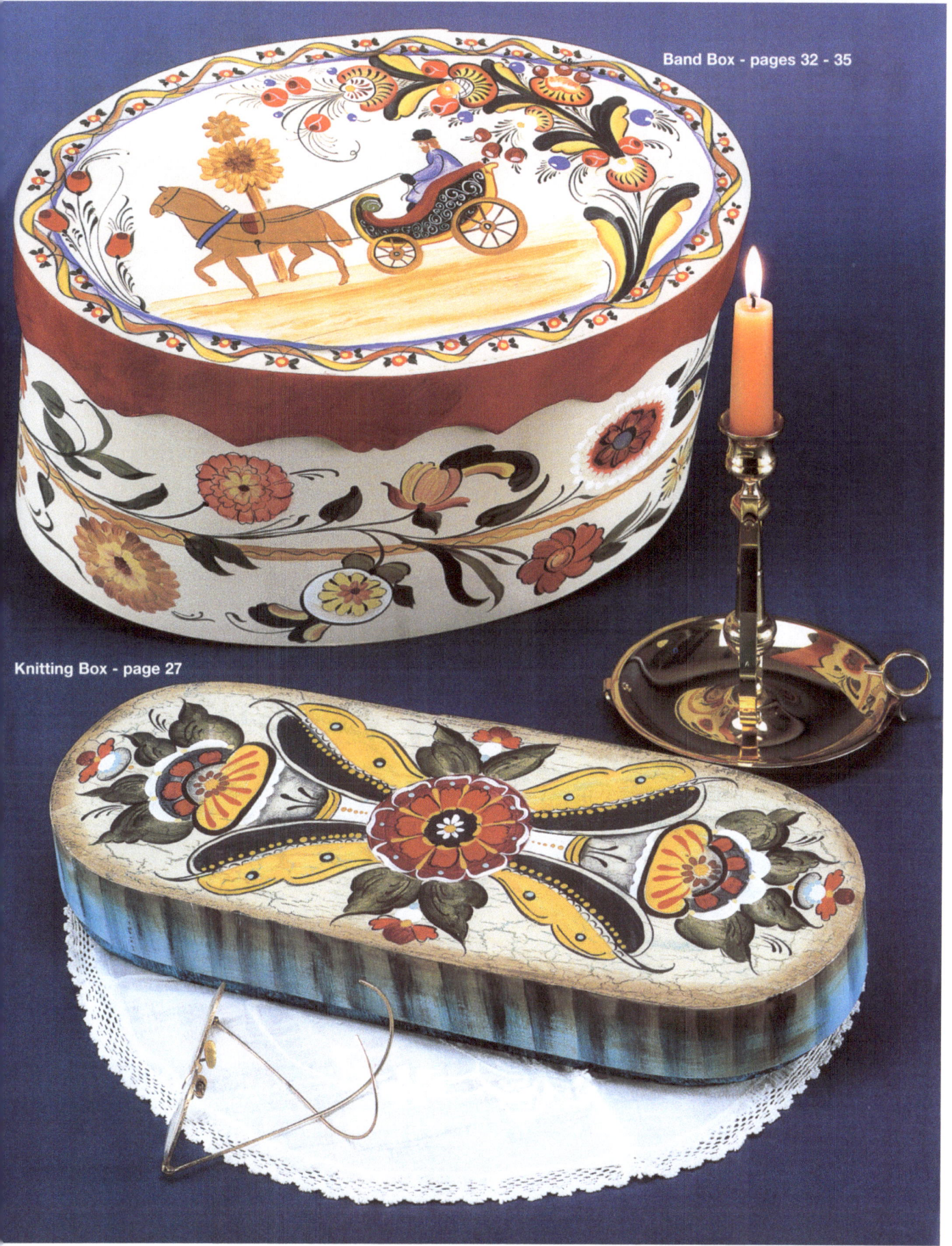

Band Box - pages 32 - 35

Knitting Box - page 27

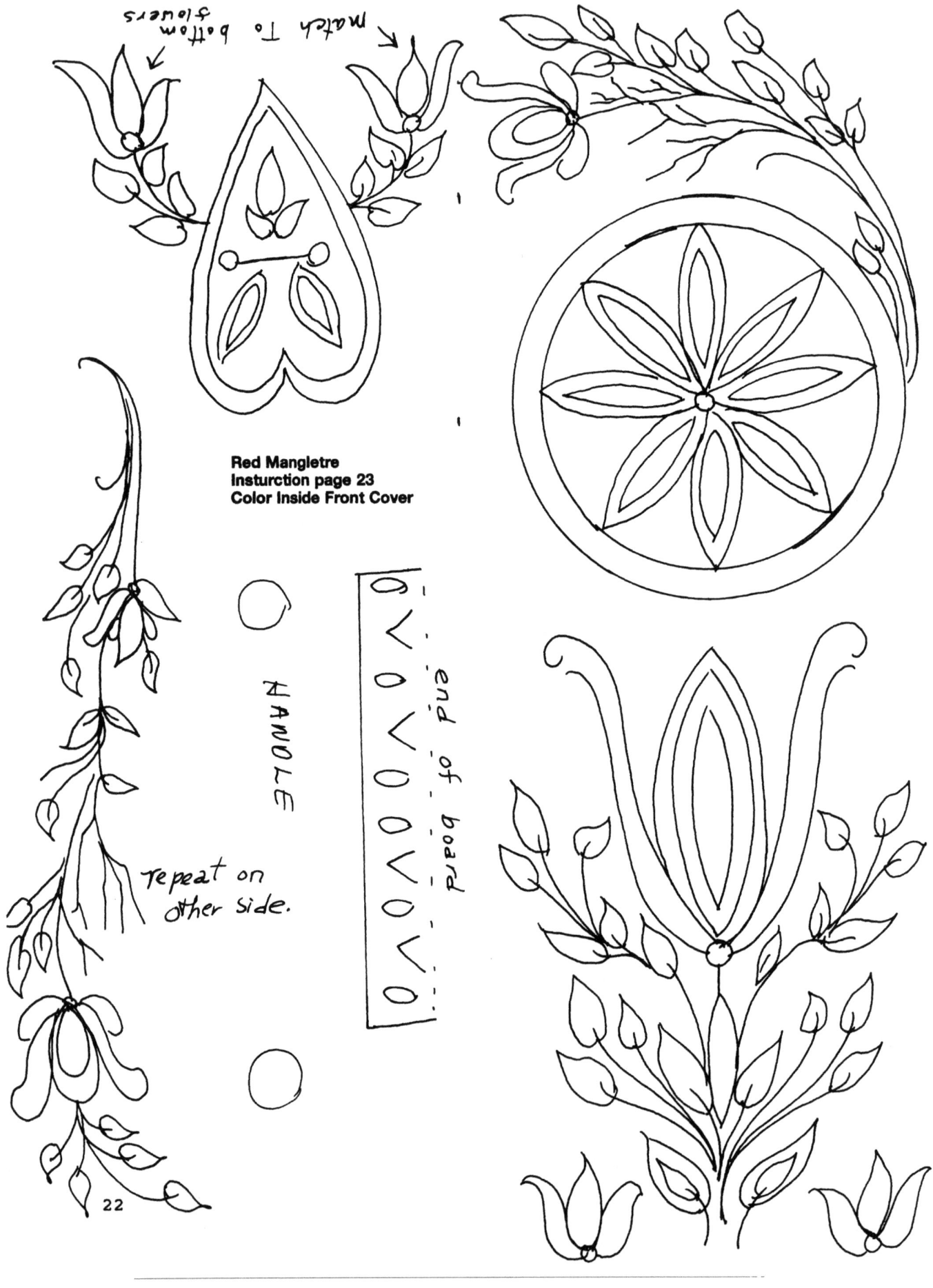

Match to bottom flowers

Red Mangletre
Insturction page 23
Color Inside Front Cover

HANDLE

repeat on other side.

end of board

22

RED MANGLETRE

Source: Valhalla Woods.
BKGD. Red Iron Oxide and Blue Haze.

The mangletre is a piece that is used to smooth out clothing which is wrapped around a large wooden dowel. In Sweden a prospective suitor often carves or paints an intricate mangle to present to his intended. Often the intended is unaware of the suitor's intentions so that some unlucky man could have quite a supply of mangles. This design came from a beautiful carved mangle that was in the Swedish Folk Art Exhibit in Santa Fe, NM. Although my carving skills are pretty limited I am always drawn to carving--maybe because my grandfather was a carpenter and carver from Norway.

Refer to the color photo. Colors used are: Hauser Dark Green, Cad. Orange, Cranberry Wine heart and circle. Center tulip is Raw Sienna, True Ochre outlined with Burnt Sienna plus Soft Black. Center is orange with Blue haze dots and RS dots on Orange. Bottom heart is outlined with BS + SB. Leaves are Blue Haze on top and True Ochre on Bottom. Raw Sienna line. Little tulips have Raw Sienna outer leaves in an S stroke with Orange center. Teardrops are Golden Straw with BS mixed with Soft Black for a deep brown. Center dots are Golden Straw with Blue Haze. Tulips on bottom are Straw, Golden Brown, BU and Orange in centers. Top tulip is Raw Sienna, Straw, Orange center with Sand teardrops. All leaves are Hauser Green Deep.

OVAL KNITTING BOX

Source: Vallhalla Woods

This box looks very old with its crackled top and antiquing. Paint with Salem Blue (a good variation of the Baltic Blue seen all over Sweden) and antique with JS Blue Glaze. Sides are done by side loading a large angle brush loaded with Retarder and JS Blue Glaze and striping down every one inch or so. Do about three strokes in a line and then reload. Shade edges of top pretty heavily. This gives a darker look under crackle. Let dry and paint top of box with a nice thick coat of DECOART Weathered Wood. Let dry overnight. Paint top only with a coat of Antique White be careful to only go one way. Use a large brush and plenty of paint with little or no water. Don't go back and fuss or you'll get a mess. Just lay paint carefully always going the same direction. Let dry.

Antique edges with 3/4" angle brush and Brown Earth Heavenly Hues. Trace on pattern with Black graphite. Start with Kurbits--Midnight Blue Deep may take two coats, leave open part in center and around edge. Paint gold side with True Ochre, keep thin and transparent. Paint all green leaves with side loaded brush, Size 8 filbert. Outline leaves with Soft Black. Large end flowers are True Ochre outlined with SB. MBD is floated on top section under red strokes and under black outlined and around the section between the Kurbits. Red petals are TR, flowers are BS petal strokes with small detail brush. Center is TO. Large teardrops are TR.

Very top flower is floated MBD with SB outline. White center surrounded by a crescent of Blue Mist dots. Side flowers are TD outlined with SB. Top flower is BS. Center dot is YO. Kurbits are finished with SB outlining and dots of TO and Large SB dots on top of gold sides. Top these when dry with a BM dot. Center flower is painted with Cranberry Wine in a large circle. Tomato Red petals are painted with Size 8 filbert. Center is painted with Midnight Blue Deep. Let dry and paint crescent strokes with white. Long True Ochre teardrops are next. Outline TR petals with SB. Center flower is White petals with a TO center dot. Blue Mist dots are inside white crescents. Refer to color photo for Black linework.

TURNED RED BOX

Source: Valhalla Woods.
BKGD: Georgia Clay mixed with JS Retarder. JS Red Glaze coated over when dry to add depth. Let the woodgrain show on beautiful pieces like this.
Teardrops on outside are True Ochre with Blue Haze + Sand dots. Center flowers are Sand with GC dots and Napa Red centers. Outside is True Ochre scalloped strokes with Soft Black lines. Midnight Blue Deep kurbits with True Ochre underneath. Dots are GC. Spinettes are True Ochre with George Clay on one side, overstroke a float of Napa Red. All lines Soft Black.

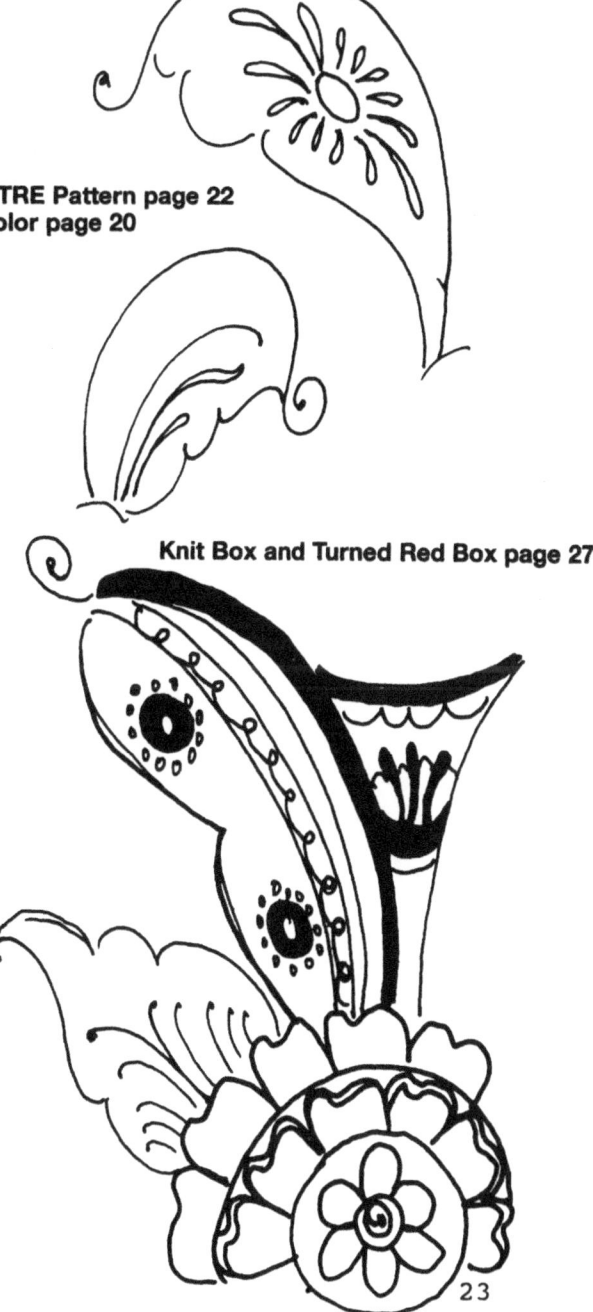

**MTRE Pattern page 22
Color page 20**

Knit Box and Turned Red Box page 27

23

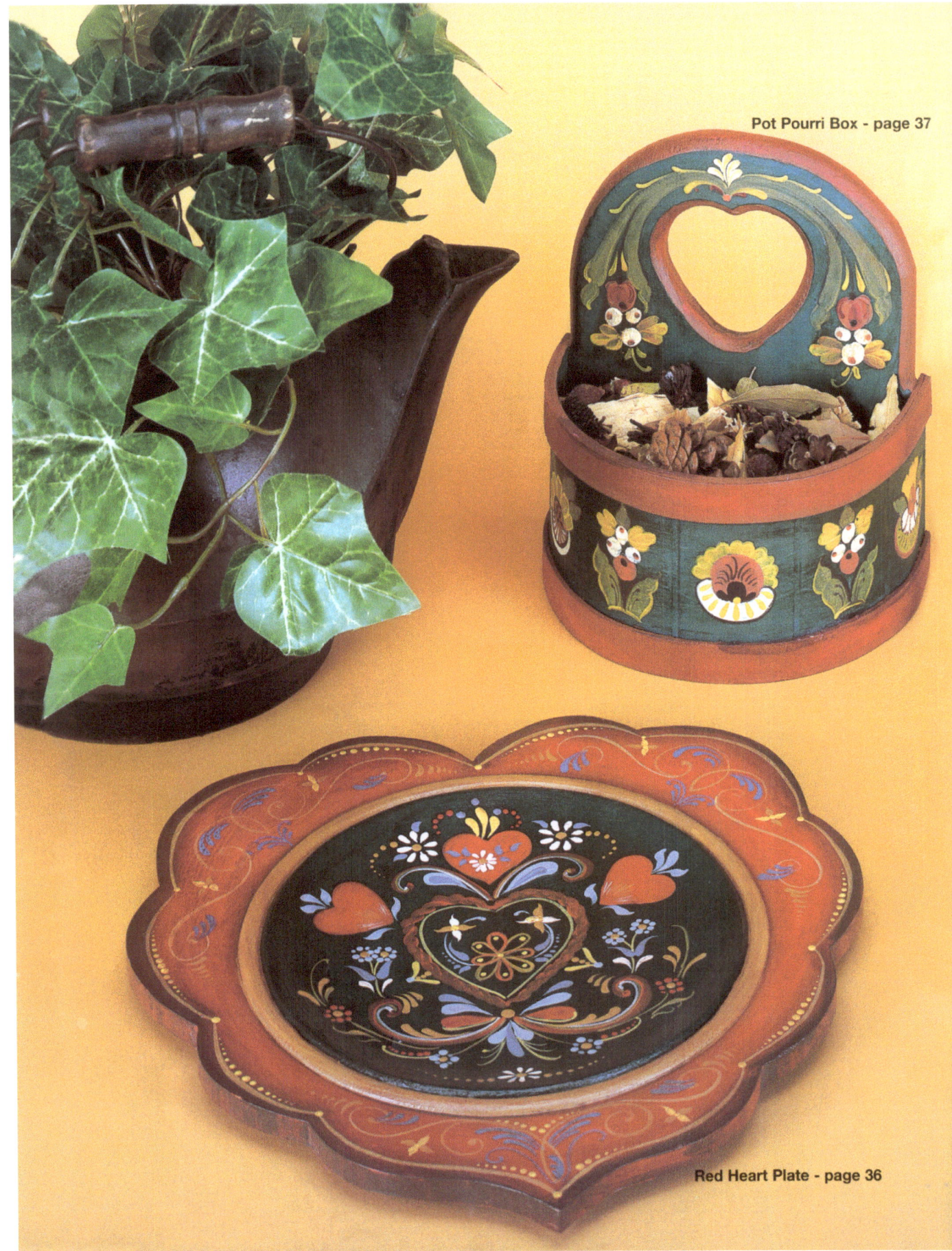

Pot Pourri Box - page 37

Red Heart Plate - page 36

Blue Heart Design Plate - page 36

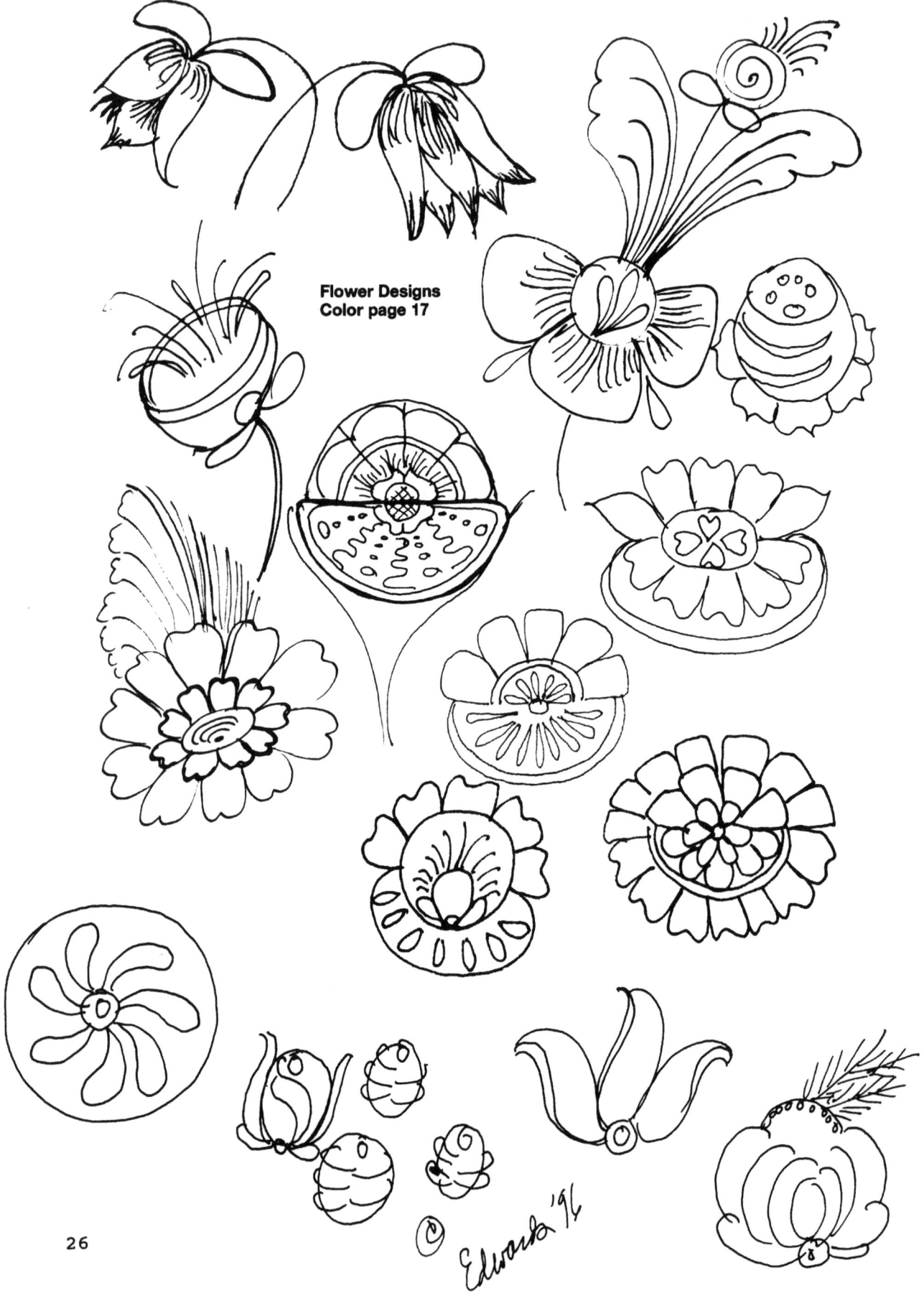

**Flower Designs
Color page 17**

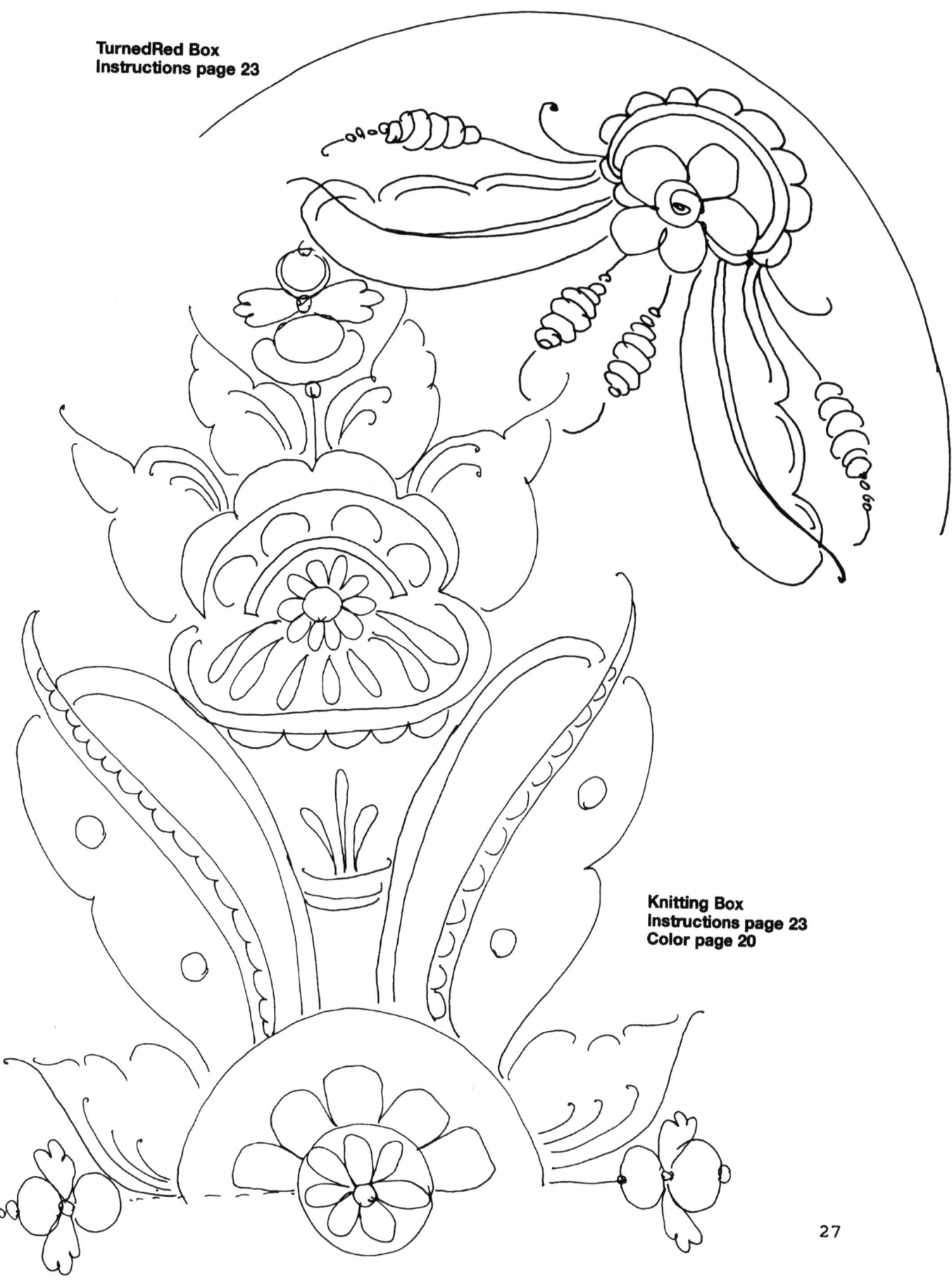

TurnedRed Box
Instructions page 23

Knitting Box
Instructions page 23
Color page 20

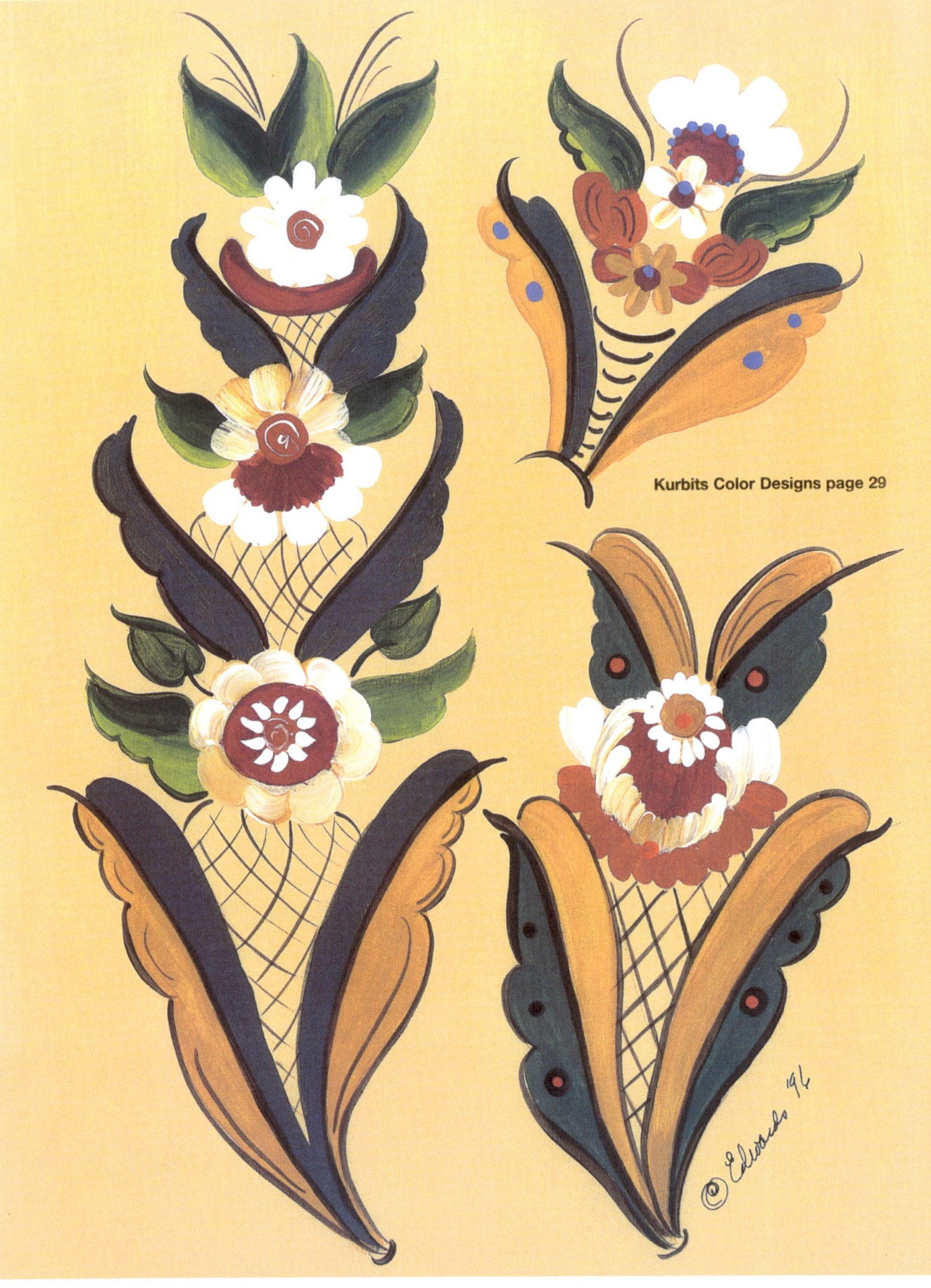

Kurbits Color Designs page 29

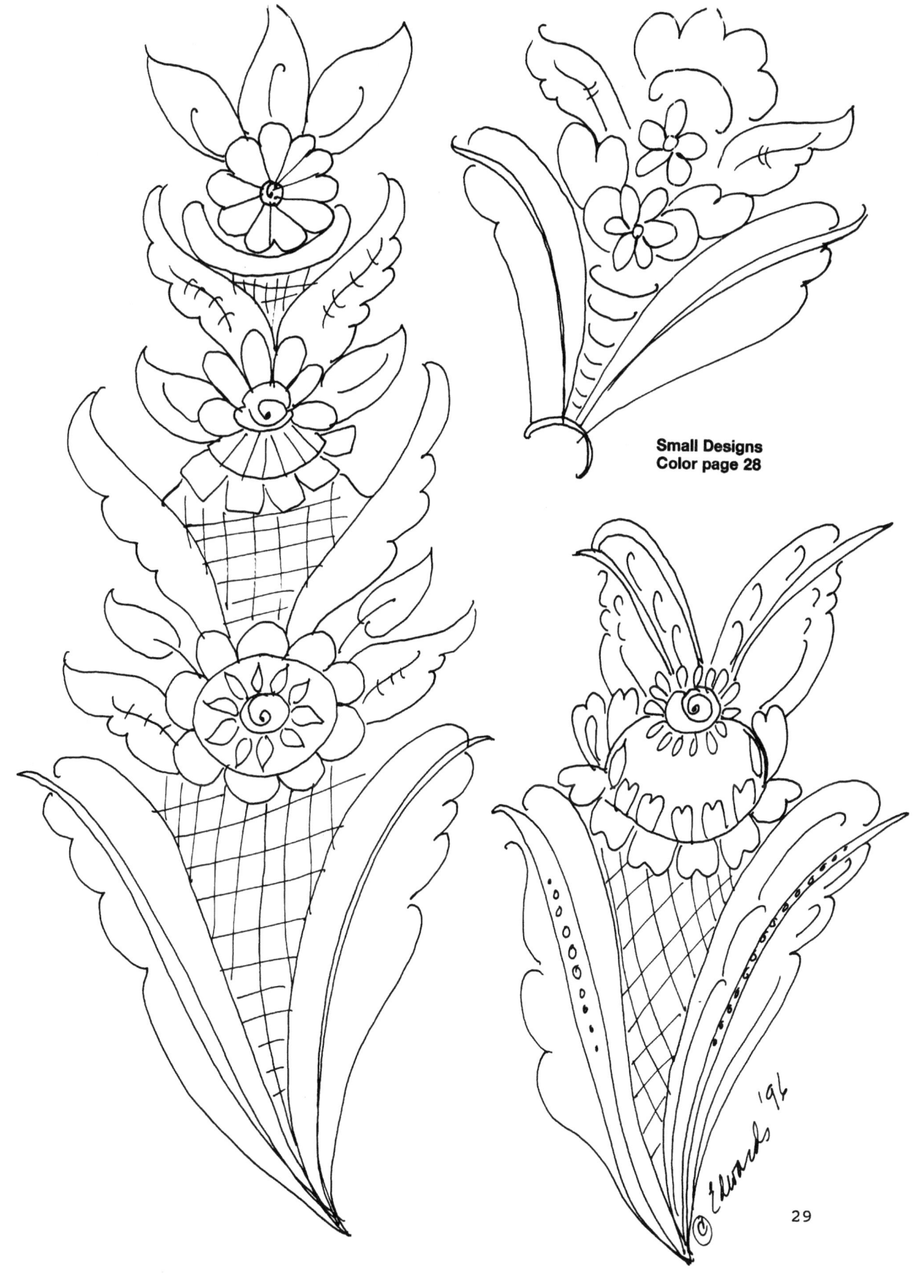

Small Designs
Color page 28

29

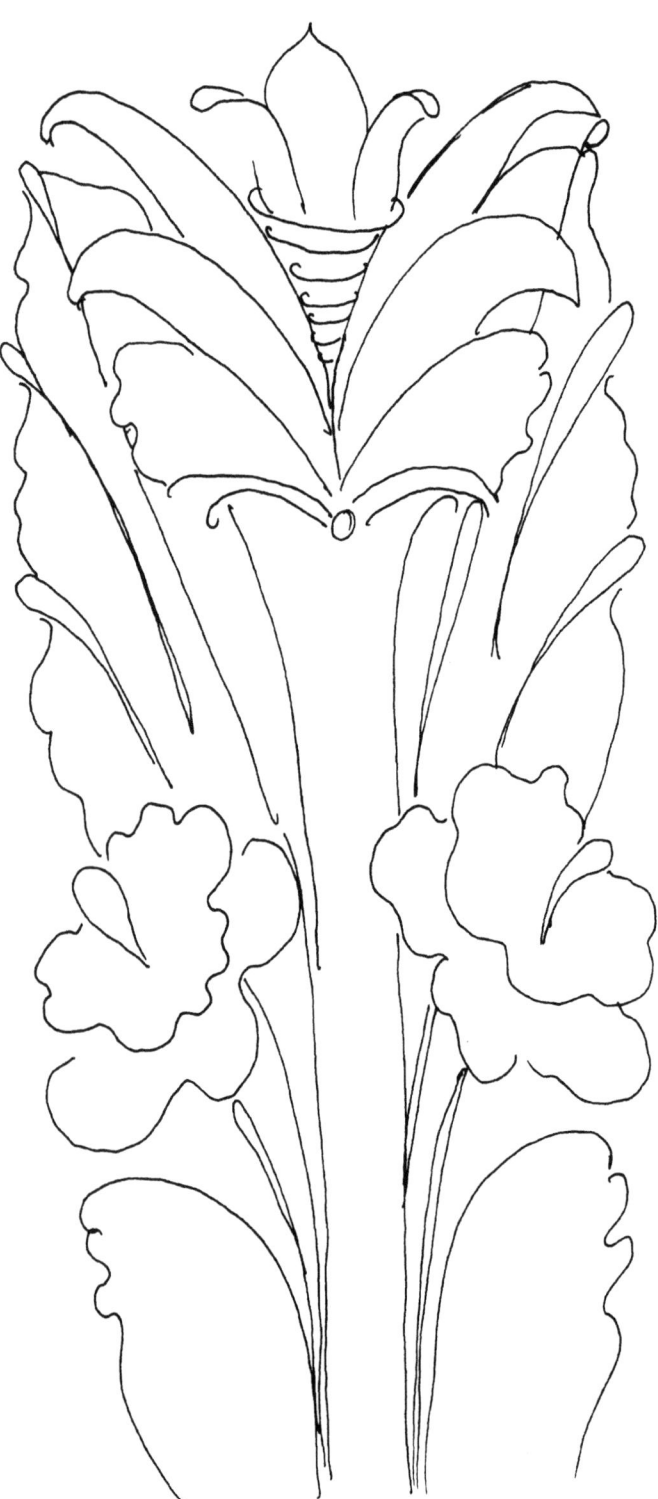

TRADITIONAL HALSINGLAND CLOCK

Source: Cabin Craft.

BKGD: Red Iron Oxide glazed with JS Red Glaze. Blue Haze glazed with JS Blue Glaze. Mix glazes with JS Kleister Medium to get the textured look and apply with an old brush. The style of this painting is the style known "compressed kurbits" often painted on wood in that area. They usually completely filled the design area. Marbling is undercoated Salem Blue. Use Kleister mixed with Blue Haze and do diagonal strokes. Touch with lines of Sand. This is, of course very artificial looking. Almost any border could be used here instead.

The side design is painted using Raw sienna on the leaf shapes edged with White. The dark red shading is Cranberry Wine. Flowers are Golden Straw edged with White on the bottom petals with Burnt Sienna edged with White. Big bottom leaves: Dark shading is Soft Black with Cranberry Wine and Golden Straw strokes. Crosshatching is Soft Black.

Front urn is Burnt Sienna with Black and True Ochre teardrops. Side teardrops and S handles are Golden Straw. Roses are painted in Cranberry Wine. Then load brush in Cranberry Wine and touch in Cad. Orange for top two roses and bottom two roses. Side roses are touched in Golden Straw. Top flower is Raw Sienna with a center dot of White and Burnt Sienna linework. All leaves are Soft Black. Center circles are Soft Black with True Ochre crescent shapes on either side. Top tulip Raw Sienna with three top petals painted Cranberry Wine edged with White. Top teardrops are Golden Straw. Center dot is Sand with a Cadmium Orange dot.

**Color Inside Front Cover
and Back Cover**

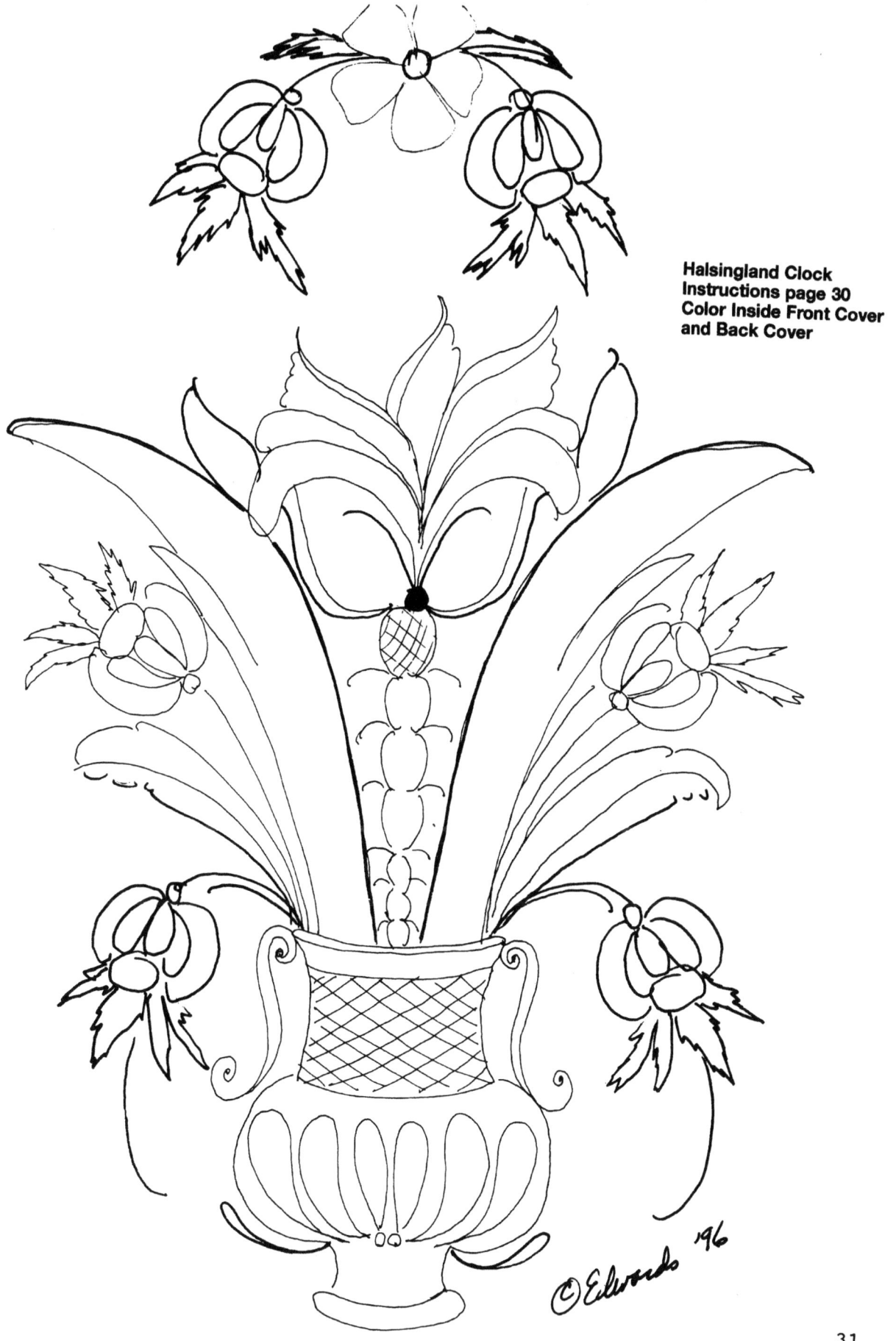

Halsingland Clock
Instructions page 30
Color Inside Front Cover
and Back Cover

©Edwards '96

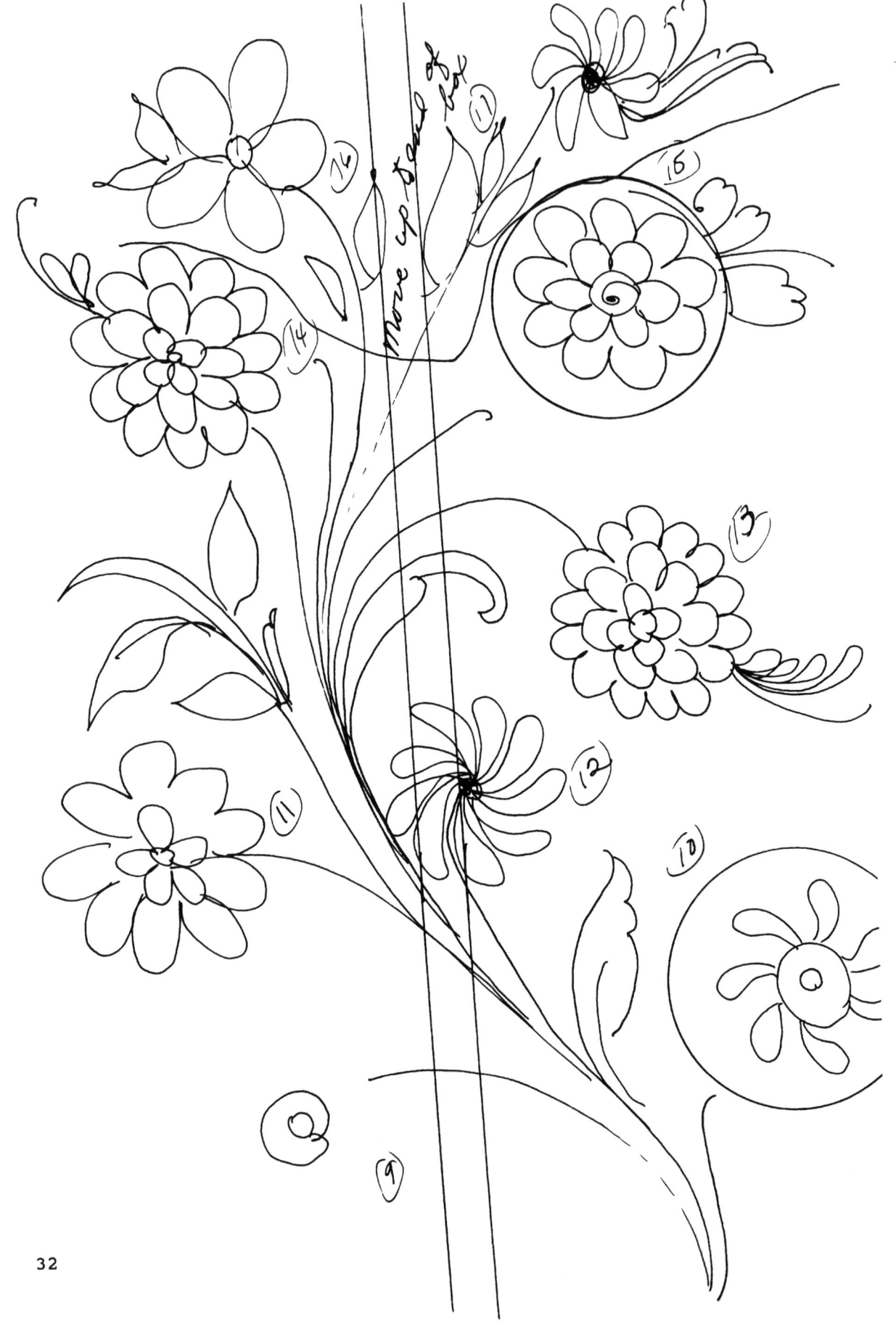

More up stand of ...

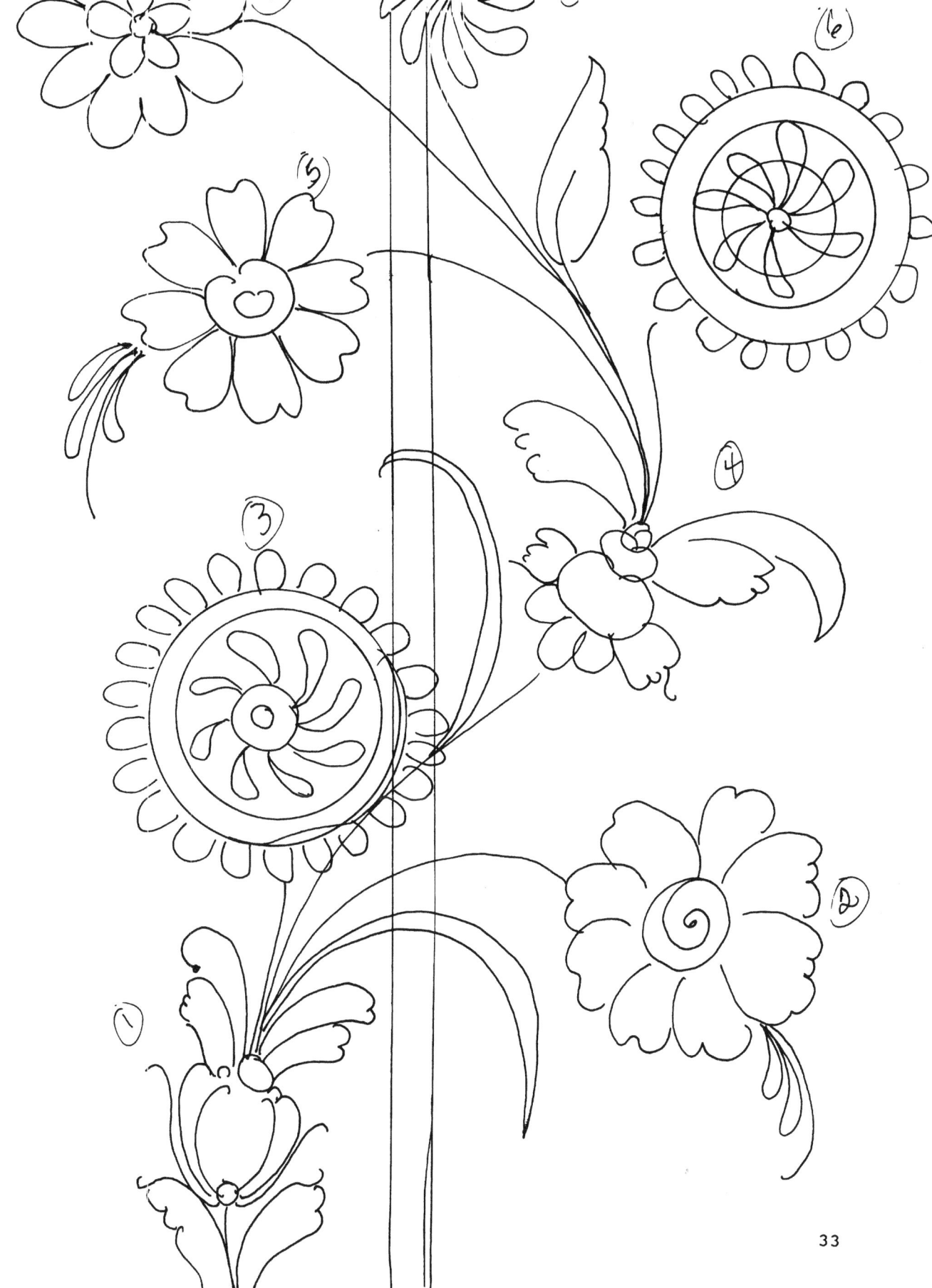

33

OVAL BAND BOX.

Source: Valhalla Woods.

This beautiful box has a stand to show it off properly. The inside of the lid can also be used as a tray. Bkgd: Antique White. Outside edge of top is Tomato Red with two coats of JS Red Glaze pounced on. The depth this gives the Tomato Red is hard to photograph but it is very beautiful.

The outside border is floated Sapphire. The ribbon is outlined with Midnight Blue Deep. Burnt Sienna on the shadowed parts and True Ochre in the front sections. Keep fairly transparent. The dots are Georgia Clay with True Ochre on top. Leaves are Hauser Green Deep. The thin line that meanders around the ribbon is very thin MBD.

HORSE AND CARRIAGE: Horse is Raw Sienna painted with two coats very solidly. Saddle is BS and collar is Sapphire. Man's coat is Sapphire painted transparently. Hat and gloves and reins are all Soft Black. The carriage is painted solidly Hauser Green Deep with Golden Straw curliques. Top edge is Napa Red and Bottom is True Ochre. Wheels are Raw Sienna outlined with RS + SB to make brown. Funny tree is painted with a Size 4 Filbert and Raw Sienna with little teardrop strokes coming inside tree. Inside of tree has some Burnt Sienna added.

KURBITS: The Blue on kurbits is Midnight Blue Deep. It takes two coats. Inside of kurbit is True Ochre shaded with Raw Sienna. All outlined with Soft Black. Crescent flowers are all similar. Paint bottom part in with Golden Straw. Georgia Clay edged with Napa Red on the bottom. Black teardrops. Top sections are White with Golden Straw dots and Napa Red Teardrops. All buds are Tomato Red with Cranberry Red dots. Darker buds are Cranberry Red with True Ochre dots. All linework on background is Hauser Green Deep.

SIDE FLOWERS: These are built up on a life line that goes around the whole box. The center band is transparent Raw Sienna with a Dark Blue line.

THE FLOWERS, starting with the flower next to the overlapping wood, are a True Ochre tulip with straw center and black outlining. The kurbits are Midnight Blue Deep, Golden Straw and Raw Sienna with a Burnt Sienna dot. Flower #2 is a White spiral flower with Raw Sienna and Golden Straw center with Cranberry Wine graduated dots. Flower #3 is painted with White outer petals, Raw Sienna floated edge onto background color, Georgia Clay circle outlined with Soft Black and Golden Straw center outlined with black. #4 is Sapphire Blue and Golden Straw center, Cranberry dots and blue and straw kurbits. #5 is Georgia Clay petals with Napa Red on one side. Center is Golden Straw with Napa Red dots. Spiral flower #6 is Raw Sienna with Golden Straw center and Napa Red dots. #7 flower is fat teardrops starting from the outside in. Load brush with Raw Sienna and tip into Burnt Sienna and start on the outside and gradually go to Golden Straw. Center is Burnt Sienna with Cranberry Wine on one side. #8 flower is Tomato Red blended with Straw moving to inside. Outlining is in Black and inside petals are Straw with a Cranberry Wine center.

Flower #9 is Sand with Straw petals, interspersed with Deep Midnight Blue. Outlined with Blue. Inside is Georgia clay petals with CW center. Leaves are HGD and HGM. Kurbits are Blue and Straw. #10 is Straw with Georgia Clay outside petals dipped in Cranberry Wine, kurbits are blue and straw. #11 is Tomato Red with Black outlining and a Straw and BS center. #12 is White with Tomato Red, Black outlining and a Sapphire Blue center oulined with Black. #13 is painted Golden Straw in a circle and blue teardrops. #14 is Straw strokes in oval with BS strokes followed by CW dots and a Straw center. #15 is Tomato Red with

Straw and BS center. #16 is White with Black outlining and True Ochre center with NR dots. #17 is a spiral flower with Tomato Red on a circle of Straw with a CW center.

Top of design for kurbits on right side of top

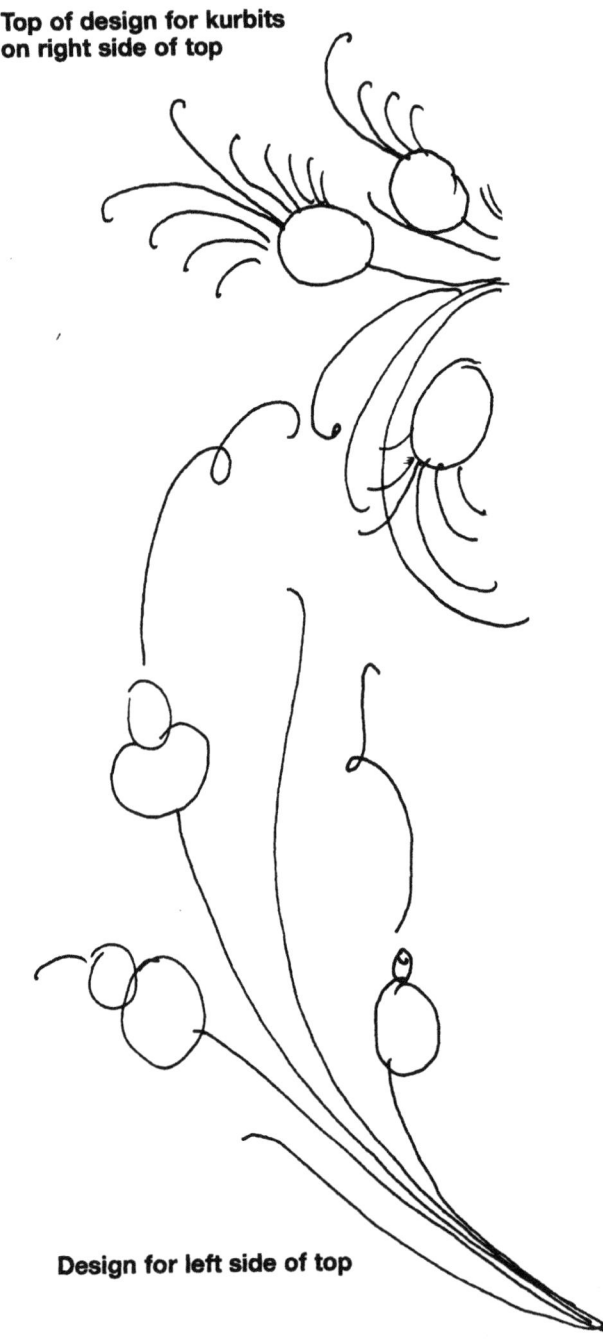

Design for left side of top

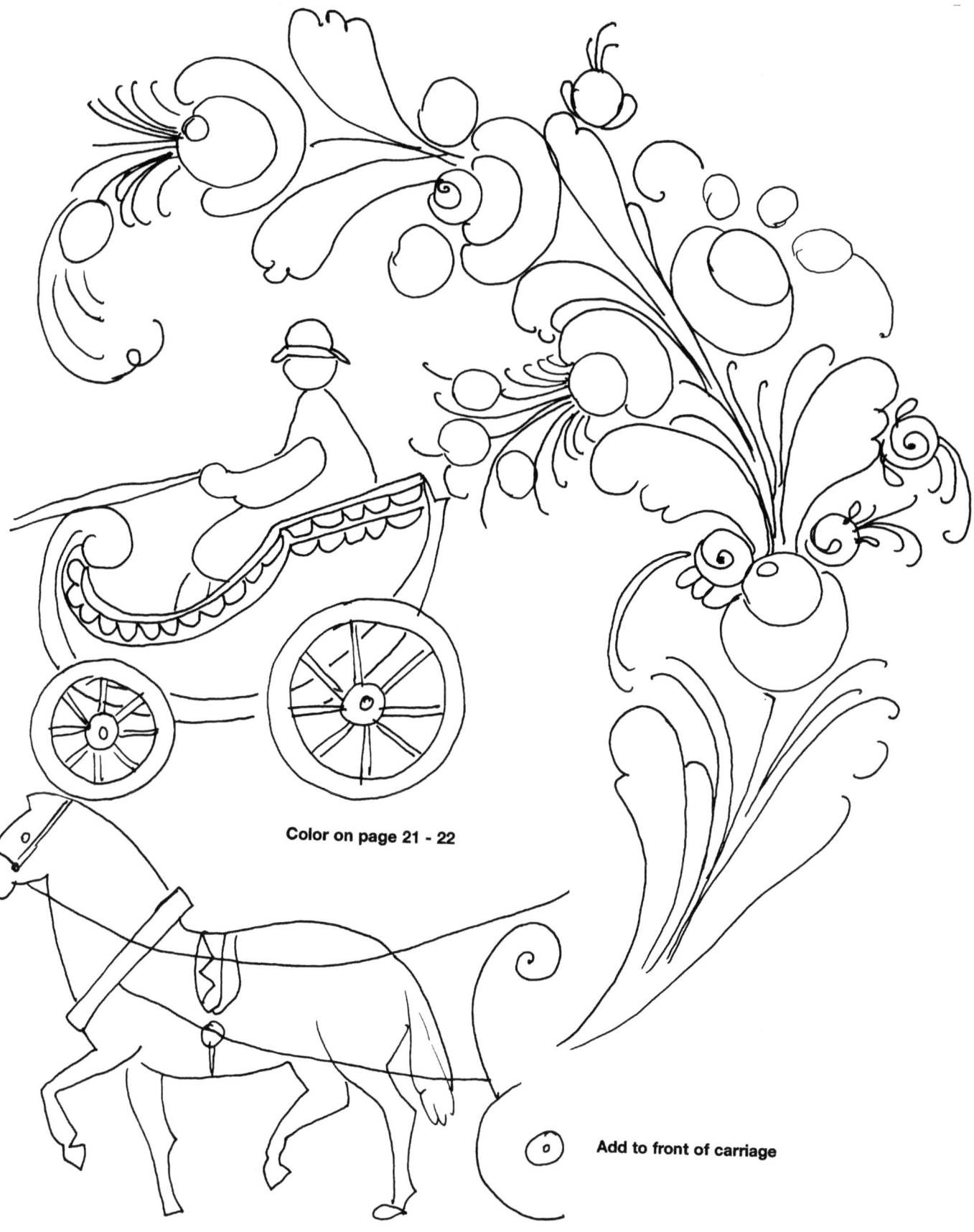

Color on page 21 - 22

Add to front of carriage

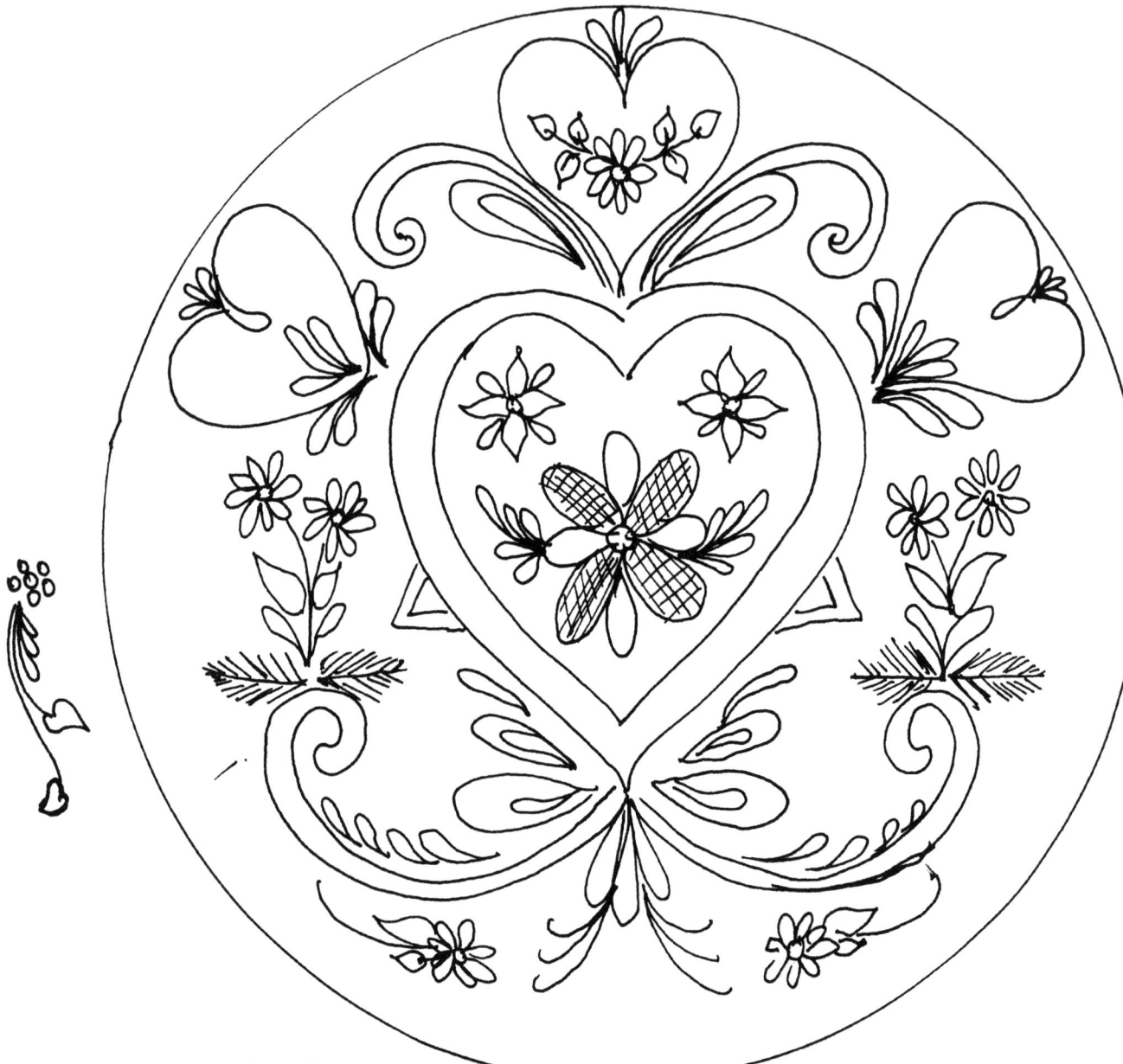

RED HEART PLATE.

SOURCE: Montzka Woodworking.
BKGD: Red Iron Oxide and Hauser Green Deep. Outside bead is Raw Sienna. Outside edge is glazed with Earth Brown. Teardrops are Blue Haze, Raw Sienna lining and True Ochre dots. Center of plate--Heart is Red Iron Oxide painted in "S" strokes with a RS inner line. Center spiral is RS and RIO, linework is Blue Haze. Top flowers are Sand and Golden Brown. Outside hearts are Tomato Red, small flowers are Sand, True Ochre teardrops on top of top heart. Blue mist teardrops and strokes on side hearts. Large teardrops under center heart are Blue Mist with Blue Haze on top. Large scrolls are Tomato Red with Sand lines inside. Raw Sienna teardrops. Side dot flowers are Tomato Red with Raw Sienna centers. Top dot flowers are Blue Mist with Raw Sienna centers. Large Blue teardrops on bottom are Blue Haze and Blue Mist. Bottom flower is Sand with Raw Sienna center and dots. RS, SAND, BLUE MIST, BLUE HAZE AND TRUE OCHRE

HEART DESIGN PLATE

Source: Montzka Woodworking.
BKGD: Blue Haze with center of Warm Neutral. Bead is Raw Sienna and S strokes are Blue Mist.

These two plates with the central heart design were developed from a design I saw on an embroidered purse. I thought this was so pretty and very "Swedish" looking so created these two plates from this design.

Center heart is Mix of Blue Mist + Blue Haze equal parts. This creates three values of Blue. Around this heart is a Raw Sienna line and a braided Tomato Red stroke. Outside of this is a Sand line going around the heart. Three hearts are Tomato Red with Raw Sienna stroke work, a Sand flower with RS center and Blue Haze teardrops or leaves. Top stroke flowers are Raw Sienna with TR centers and Blue Haze leaves. Large scroll strokes are red with Raw Sienna inside, Blue Haze lines with a teardrop and Blue Mist large teardrops with the Blue Mix on top. Bottom scrolls are TR with Sand lines inside and RS teardrops. Three blue colors are Dark--Blue Haze, Medium--Blue Mix and Light--Blue Mist. Side flowers are Raw Sienna, Sand and TR center dots. Leaves and teardrops are Blue Haze.

HANGING HEART HOLDER:

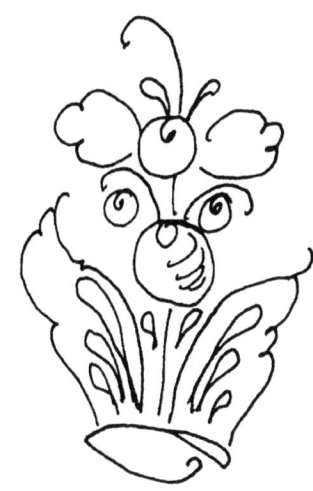

I found this at a local craft shop--it is pretty rustic but after sanding forever, I took JB, ETC., Wood Putty and filled in everything with my fingers. This helped considerably and, although you can't stain such a piece, it really smooths it out.

Background is Hauser Green Deep with Red Iron Oxide on the edges. I glazed the edges several times with JS Red Glaze to give them a little more depth. Top leaves or "kurbits" are Hauser Green Medium with True Ochre teardrops. Center teardrops are Golden Straw. Bottom teardrops are True Ochre and Red Iron Oxide with a Georgia Clay dot. Roses are Georgia Clay with RIO teardrops and Cranberry Wine dots. Sand roses have GC dots. Leaf forms are made with a Size 2 Filbert dipped in Red Iron Oxide and then in True Ochre. Push down and lift up. Bottom lines are teardrops are TO. Flowers around the bottom section are interspersed with a small plant form. Plant leaves are HGM outlined on one side with SB and on other with TO. Flowers are as above.

LARGE FLOWERS: on left the flower is painted Georgia Clay in the center with Black and Sand teardrops and outlining. Large petals are True Ochre and leaves are HGM. Center flower is Georgia Clay with Cranberry Wine petals and lines. Bottom crescent is Sand and top petals are TO. Last flower is painted True Ochre on crescent with outline of RIO and Black. Center crescent is Sand with Cranberry Wine outlining. Top section is TO with HGM leaves. The center four petal flower is RIO.

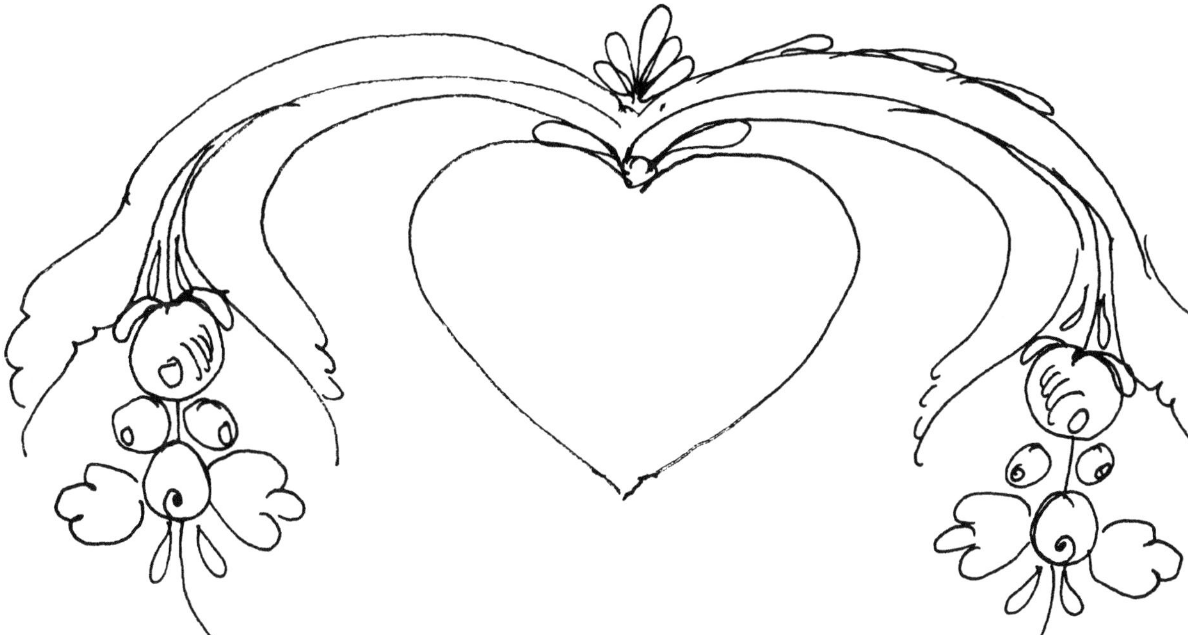

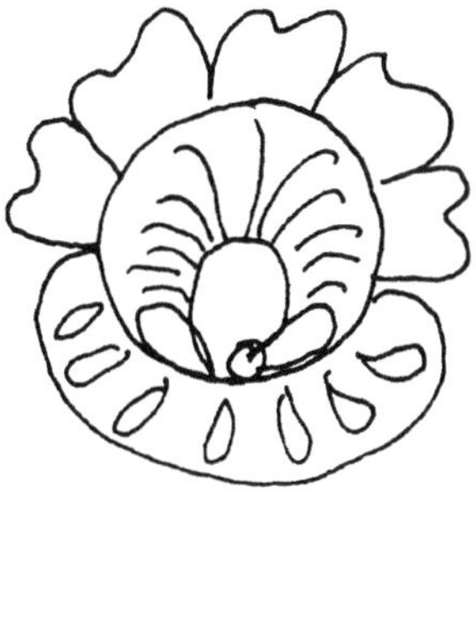

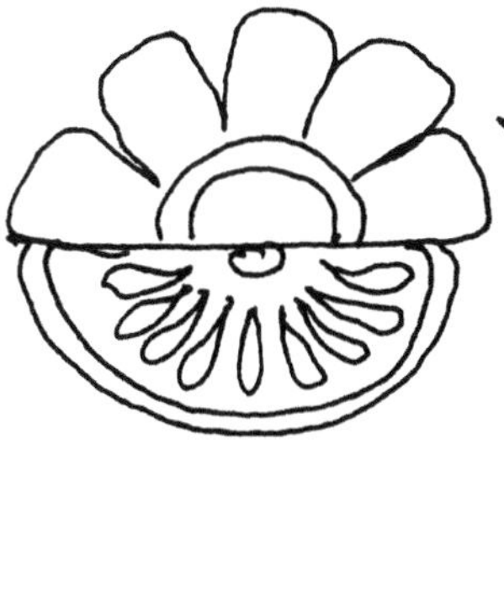

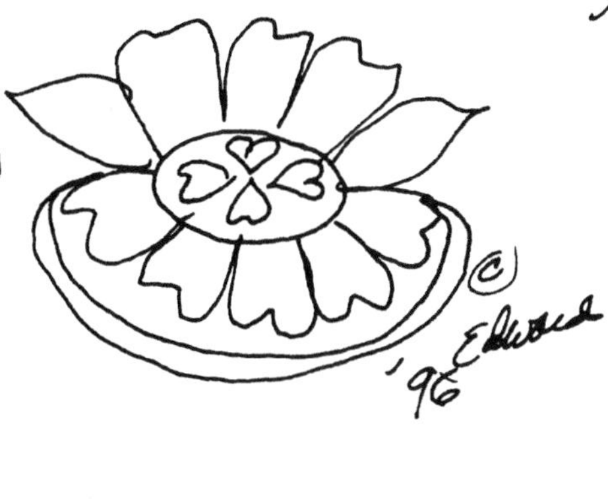

'96

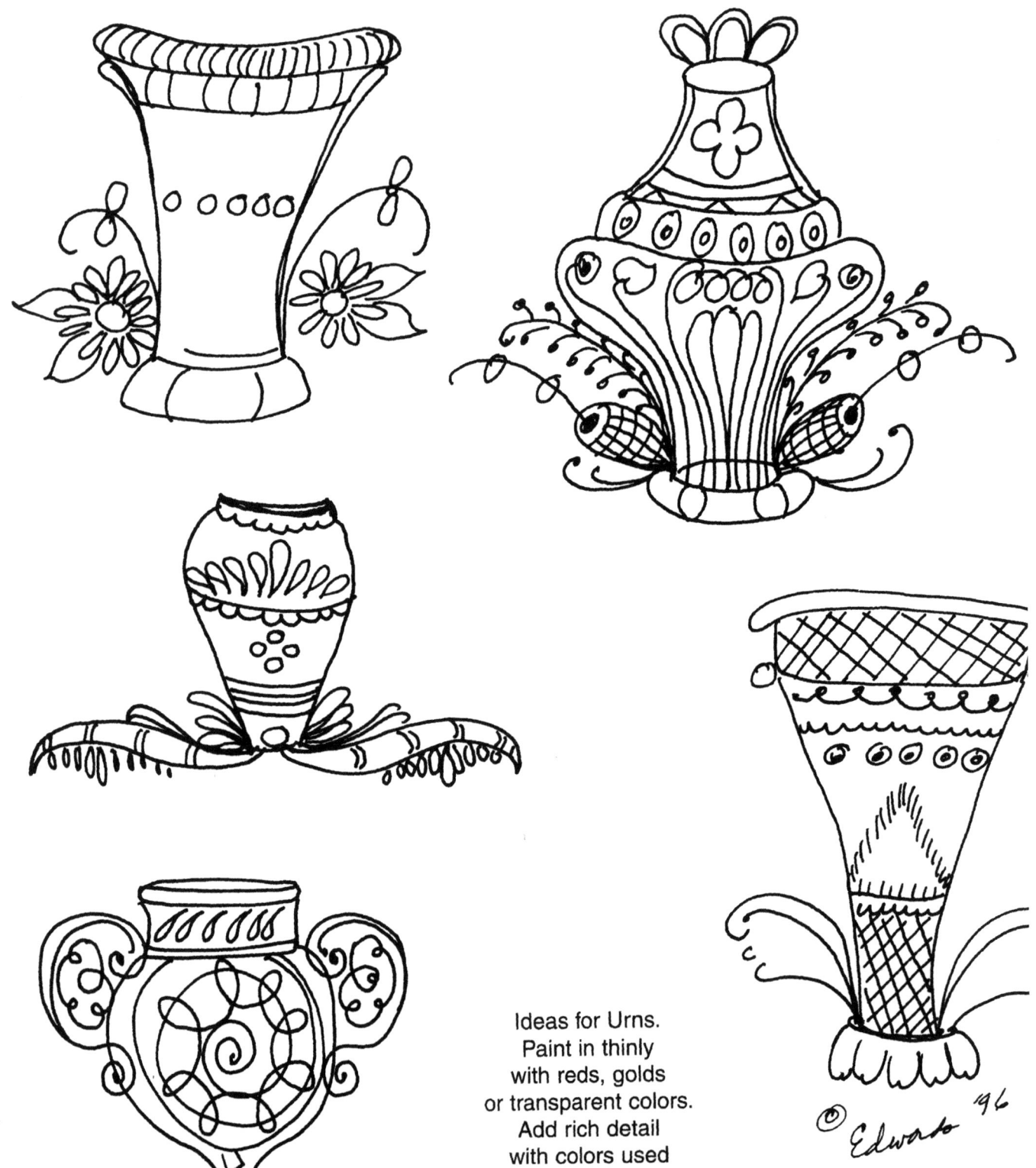

Ideas for Urns.
Paint in thinly
with reds, golds
or transparent colors.
Add rich detail
with colors used
in the rest of the
design.

© Edwards '96

38

SUPPLIES

<u>Paints listed as equivalents to acrylics listed below.</u>
<u>Oil Paints</u>
1) Titanium White
2) Yellow Ochre
3) Prussian Blue
+ Burnt Umber =pts
4) English Red Light
5) Burnt Umber
6) Burnt Sienna
7) Raw Sienna
8) Ivory Black
9) Prussian Blue + Burnt Sienna
= pts + 1/2 pt Tit. White
10) Viridian
11) Alizarin Crimson

MEDIUMS--
Pale Drying Oil
Odorless Mineral Spirits

<u>Acrylics</u>
1) Titanium White-JS and Deco
2) Yellow Oxide-JS
   True Ochre-Deco
3) Storm Blue--JS
   Midnight Blue Deep--Deco
4) Red Earth-JS
   Red Iron Oxide--Deco
5) Burnt Umber--JS and Deco
6) Burnt Sienna--JS and Deco
7) Raw Sienna--JS and Deco
8) Carbon Black--JS
   Soft Black--Deco
9) Sapphire + Teal Green--JS
   Blue Haze--Deco
10) Pine Green-JS
    Hauser Dark Green--Deco
11) Burgundy--JS
    Cranberry Wine--Deco

MEDIUMS:
JoSonja--Retarder, Flow Medium, Kleister Medium and Clear Glaze Medium for sealer and glazing.
Backgrounds--Mix JS paints with All Purpose Sealer
 Use Tannin Sealer for dark spots, knotholes, etc.
DecoArt--Brush 'n Blend

Control Medium

GLAZES:
DECOART HEAVENLY HUES--Brown Earth for antiquing and glazing. JS--Blue, Yellow and Red. Clear Glaze.
OTHER SUPPLIES--
Strip palette, palette knife (I prefer a Langnickel P1), Stabilo pencil for designing and borders, containers for mediums and water, sponge brushes for background paints, small plastic bags to hold wet sponge brushes, paper towels, sandpaper.
BRUSHES
Silver brush Golden Natural. Golden Natural is a blend of animal hair and taklon that will work in both oil and water based paints.
Filberts, Series 2003S--sizes 2, 4, 6, 8 and 10, A size 6 will be fine to start.
Liners, Size 0 and 1--Series 2005S
Script, Size 0 and 1--Series 2007S
VARNISHES
Oil Base--Benjamin Moore One Hour Quick Finish in Low Lustre (dries in one hour)
Water Base
JW Right Step Matte or Satin. Two coats are preferable.
Varnish Brush--1" wash brush, Series 2008S Silver Brush

Materials needed for finishing: Use damp paper towel to wipe off sanding dust.
   3M sanding sponge and finishing pads in different grades.

PICKLING--Use JW's White Lightning and add DecoArt paint until correct shade is achieved. Be careful to apply with a large enough brush and go with the grain. I use a wash brush as listed above in 3/4" or 1". (Don't use the same brush for varnishing. Buy two!! For side loading JS glazes I prefer a 3/4" angle brush such as Silver Brush Series 2006S.

Bibliography:

Biblia Dalecarlica by Svante Svardstrom.
Dalmalmingar i Urval by Svante Svardstrom. 1957
Dalmalningar I Zornmuseet by Svante Svardstrom. 1957
Blommande allmogemaleri by Lena Nessle. 2002
Dalmalningar I jamforande perspektiv by many authors. 1992 (wall painting)
The Decorative Arts of Sweden by Iona Plath. 1966. Dover
Decorativ Mogel Malning by Annie Sloan. 1989 Raben & Sjogren
Gamle Mobler. Mobelstilar och inredning i Sverige 1700-1950. by Jane Fredlund. 1995 Ica Bokforlag.
The Magic Horse by Chris Mosey and Michel Hjorth. 1999. BOOX Stockholm
Malade Allmogemobler by Jane Fredlund 1989 Ica Bokforlag Vasteras.
Skansen. Traditional Swedish Style. 1995 Scala Books.
The Swedish Room by Lars Sjoberg. 2000 Pantheon Books.
Lars Bolander's Scandinavian Design By Heather MacIsaac. 2010

Websites:
www.nordic-arts.com
www.DianeEdwardsArt.com
www.Ingebretsens.com
www.skansen.se/org
www.dalarnasmuseum.se.org
www.nordicworld.com
www.blondell.com
  Swedish Antiques
www.vesterheim.org
Norwegian American Museum
www.americanswedishinst.org
Swedish Institute in Minneapolis
www.scandiamn.com
Gammelgarden Museum in Minnesota
www.skandisk.com

Sources for wood:

Lusk Scandia Woodworks, cupboards, Trunks, unusual Nordic pieces
www.luskscandiawoodworks.com
Turn of the Century Wood Products
Beautiful plates and bowls
www.turnofthecentury-in-com
Turns In Time, Ltd.
Plates, bowls, stools, etc.
www.turnsintime.com
Norwegian Woods, Cupboards, bowls
www.atouchofnordic.com
Viking Woodcrafts Supplies
www.vikingwoodcrafts.com
Norsk Woodworks, carving
www.norskwoodworks.com
Hofcraft, Wood and Paint Supplies
www.Hofcraft.com
Rosemal Wood,Beautiful Tines
www.rosemalwood.com
Norskedalen Heritage Wood
www.JoanneMacvey.com/home/wooden ware.htm

BOOKS BY DIANE EDWARDS
1,2 Design Basics for Telemark Rosemaling,
Volumes I and II
3. Rosemaling Boxes
Norwegian Rosemaling for Young People
4. Aarseth's Rosemaling Design
by Diane Edwards and Sigmund Aarseth
5. Painted Rooms by Gudmund Aarseth
6. Swedish Folk Art,
Floral and Kurbits Designs
(2005, 88 Pages, patterns)

Published by:
Nordic Arts www.nordic-arts.com
3208 Snowbrush Place
Fort Collins, CO 80521
970-229-9846
Orders welcomed.
www.nordic-arts.com

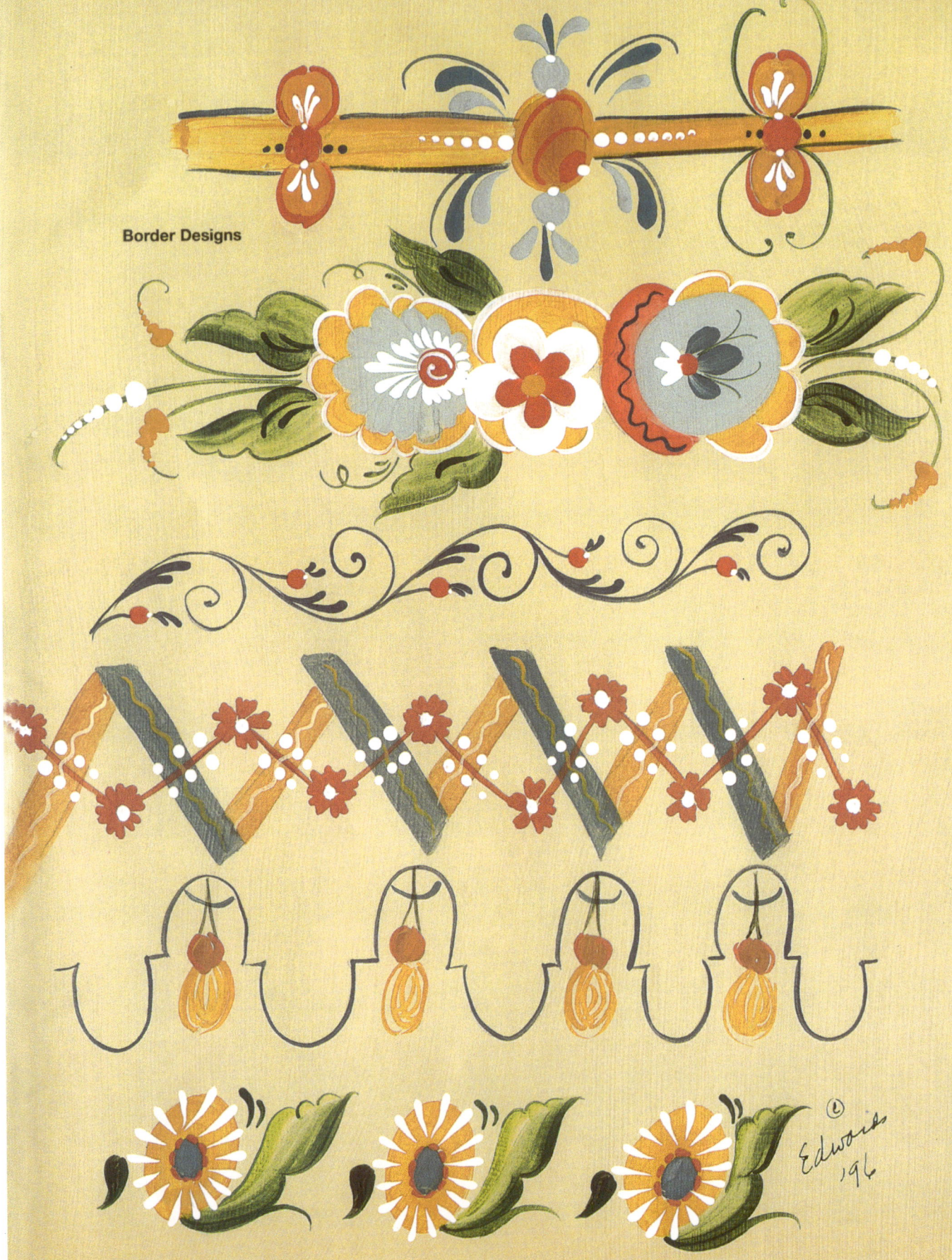

Border Designs

Edwards '96